The Arapaho

Indians of North America

Heritage Edition

◀Indians▶
of North
America

The Apache

The Arapaho

The Blackfeet

The Cherokees

The Cheyenne

The Choctaw

The Comanche

The Hopi

The Iroquois

The Mohawk

The Navajo

The Pawnee

The Teton Sioux

The Zuni

Heritage Edition

Indians of North America

The Arapaho

Loretta Fowler

Foreword by
Ada E. Deer
University of Wisconsin-Madison

CHELSEA HOUSE PUBLISHERS

COVER: An Arapaho parfleche, used to transport household articles and food-stuffs.

CHELSEA HOUSE PUBLISHERS

VP, NEW PRODUCT DEVELOPMENT   Sally Cheney
DIRECTOR OF PRODUCTION   Kim Shinners
CREATIVE MANAGER   Takeshi Takahashi
MANUFACTURING MANAGER   Diann Grasse

Staff for THE ARAPAHO

EXECUTIVE EDITOR   Lee Marcott
EDITOR   Christian Green
PRODUCTION EDITOR   Bonnie Cohen
PHOTO EDITOR   Sarah Bloom
SERIES AND COVER DESIGNER   Keith Trego
LAYOUT   EJB Publishing Services

www.chelseahouse.com

First Printing

9 8 7 6 5 4 3 2 1

Library of Congress Cataloging-in-Publication Data

Fowler, Loretta, 1944-
  The Arapaho / Loretta Fowler.— Heritage ed.
    p. cm. — (Indians of North America)
  Includes bibliographical references and index.
  ISBN 0-7910-8593-7 (hard cover)
  1. Arapaho Indians—Juvenile literature. I. Title. II. Indians of North America
(Chelsea House Publishers)
  E99.A7F677 2005
  978.004'97354—dc22
                                    2005008830

Contents

Foreword

Ada E. Deer

American Indians are an integral part of our nation's life and history. Yet most Americans think of their Indian neighbors as stereotypes; they are woefully uninformed about them as fellow humans. They know little about the history, culture, and contributions of Native people. In this new millennium, it is essential for every American to know, understand, and share in our common heritage. The Cherokee teacher, the Mohawk steelworker, and the Ojibwe writer all express their tribal heritage while living in mainstream America.

The revised INDIANS OF NORTH AMERICA series, which focuses on some of the continent's larger tribes, provides the reader with an accurate perspective that will better equip him/her to live and work in today's world. Each tribe has a unique history and culture, and knowledge of individual tribes is essential to understanding the Indian experience.

Prior to the arrival of Columbus in 1492, scholars estimate the Native population north of the Rio Grande ranged from seven to twenty-five million people who spoke more than three hundred different languages. It has been estimated that ninety percent of the Native population was wiped out by disease, war, relocation, and starvation. Today there are more than 567 tribes, which have a total population of more than two million. When Columbus arrived in the Bahamas, the Arawak Indians greeted him with gifts, friendship, and hospitality. He noted their ignorance of guns and swords and wrote they could easily be overtaken with fifty men and made to do whatever he wished. This unresolved clash in perspectives continues to this day.

A holistic view recognizing the connections of all people, the land, and animals pervades the life and thinking of Native people. These core values—respect for each other and all living things; honoring the elders; caring, sharing, and living in balance with nature; and using not abusing the land and its resources—have sustained Native people for thousands of years.

American Indians are recognized in the U.S. Constitution. They are the only group in this country who has a distinctive *political* relationship with the federal government. This relationship is based on the U.S. Constitution, treaties, court decisions, and attorney-general opinions. Through the treaty process, millions of acres of land were ceded *to* the U.S. government *by* the tribes. In return, the United States agreed to provide protection, health care, education, and other services. All 377 treaties were broken by the United States. Yet treaties are the supreme law of the land as stated in the U.S. Constitution and are still valid. Treaties made more than one hundred years ago uphold tribal rights to hunt, fish, and gather.

Since 1778, when the first treaty was signed with the Lenni-Lenape, tribal sovereignty has been recognized and a government-to-government relationship was established. This concept of tribal power and authority has continuously been

misunderstood by the general public and undermined by the
states. In a series of court decisions in the 1830s, Chief Justice
John Marshall described tribes as "domestic dependent
nations." This status is not easily understood by most people
and is rejected by state governments who often ignore and/or
challenge tribal sovereignty. Sadly, many individual Indians and
tribal governments do not understand the powers and limita-
tions of tribal sovereignty. An overarching fact is that Congress
has plenary, or absolute, power over Indians and can exercise
this sweeping power at any time. Thus, sovereignty is tenuous.

Since the July 8, 1970, message President Richard Nixon
issued to Congress in which he emphasized "self-determination without termination," tribes have re-emerged and have
utilized the opportunities presented by the passage of major
legislation such as the American Indian Tribal College Act
(1971), Indian Education Act (1972), Indian Education and
Self-Determination Act (1975), American Indian Health Care
Improvement Act (1976), Indian Child Welfare Act (1978),
American Indian Religious Freedom Act (1978), Indian Gaming
Regulatory Act (1988), and Native American Graves Preservation
and Repatriation Act (1990). Each of these laws has enabled tribes
to exercise many facets of their sovereignty and consequently has
resulted in many clashes and controversies with the states and the
general public. However, tribes now have more access to and can
afford attorneys to protect their rights and assets.

Under provisions of these laws, many Indian tribes reclaimed
power over their children's education with the establishment of
tribal schools and thirty-one tribal colleges. Many Indian children have been rescued from the foster-care system. More tribal
people are freely practicing their traditional religions. Tribes with
gaming revenue have raised their standard of living with
improved housing, schools, health clinics, and other benefits.
Ancestors' bones have been reclaimed and properly buried. All of
these laws affect and involve the federal, state, and local governments as well as individual citizens.

Tribes are no longer people of the past. They are major players in today's economic and political arenas; contributing millions of dollars to the states under the gaming compacts and supporting political candidates. Each of the tribes in INDIANS OF NORTH AMERICA demonstrates remarkable endurance, strength, and adaptability. They are buying land, teaching their language and culture, and creating and expanding their economic base, while developing their people and making decisions for future generations. Tribes will continue to exist, survive, and thrive.

Ada E. Deer
University of Wisconsin–Madison
June 2004

1

Devotees and Prophets

In the beginning, according to Arapaho accounts, the First Pipe Keeper floated on a limitless body of water with the Flat Pipe. He fasted and prayed to the Creator, who inspired him to send the duck to search beneath the water's surface. The duck emerged with a little bit of dirt, which the First Pipe Keeper put on the Pipe. Then he sent the turtle to the bottom, and it, too, returned with dirt. The First Pipe Keeper put this dirt on the Pipe and blew it all off toward each of the four directions. In doing so, he created the earth. Then he made the sun and moon, man and woman, and vegetable and animal life, followed by day and night and the four seasons. He then taught the first people the religious rites that they would need. The duck and turtle were placed with the Pipe into a bundle, and the Arapahos—descendants of that first man and woman—have been responsible for them ever since. For the Arapahos the contents of the bundle are symbols of the creation, and their custody of the bundle a sacred trust.[1]

The Arapahos believed that supernatural power, and the life force itself, emanated from the Creator, or from the "Great Mystery Above." During mythological times, the Creator infused this power into other beings—forces of nature, animals, and some minerals. The Arapahos could appeal to these supernatural beings for help. The Creator's power on earth was first and foremost manifest in the Flat Pipe. The sacred bundle from the creation story was a medium through which prayers were conveyed to the Creator.

James Mooney, an ethnologist with the Smithsonian Institution, in Washington, D.C., wrote in 1890 that the Arapahos were an intensely religious people, "devotees and prophets, continually seeing signs and wonders." The Arapahos believed that religious devotion would be rewarded with help from the Creator in achieving health, happiness, and success. If they gave the Creator proper respect, prayer, and supplication, then cosmic, natural, and social forces would operate harmoniously. Elderly people had primary responsibility for maintaining good relations with the Creator, and people sought their assistance in petitioning for supernatural aid.[2]

All adults exerted much effort in communicating with the Creator through prayer, or earnest "wish thought." They prayed often, using pipes, smoke, steam, or song to convey their prayers to the Creator above. Sacrifice, in the form of offerings, was believed to express the supplicant's sincerity and frequently accompanied prayer. Offerings might include food (often presented as gifts to elders), tobacco or a filled pipe, property, or even the sacrifice of a finger joint or a bit of flesh.

Arapaho stories about the *tribe's* past credit heroes with showing the people how to thrive in the world. Through supernatural aid these heroes made important discoveries and performed extraordinary deeds. One hero taught the Arapahos how to make an enclosure near a cliff to trap buffalo, and how to catch and train horses. Another discovered how to make and use bone tools: the first arrowhead (from the rib of a buffalo)

This 1910 photo taken by renowned Native American photographer Edward Curtis shows an Arapaho man smoking a pipe. Smoking tobacco was a means by which the Arapahos conveyed their prayers to the Creator.

and the first bow—both technological advances that made hunting easier—and how to use stone to shape a knife made from the shoulder blade of a buffalo. A third invented a more efficient way of making fire by striking flint rather than using a drill. The Arapahos' major ceremonies were also believed to have originated in individuals' encounters with supernatural beings.[3]

In the 1840s, the Arapahos were well known to pioneers

Like many Plains Indians, the Arapahos used the *travois* to transport their possessions when they moved their camps. Originally pulled by dogs and later by horses,
this device consisted of two poles that were tied together around the animal's shoulders and contained either straps or wooden crosspieces that were laid between the
poles to hold the Arapahos' goods (or children, as shown here).

crossing the *Great Plains*, but when—and from where—the
Arapahos moved into the area is still uncertain. They were
probably living on the northern plains near the headwaters of
the Missouri River before the eighteenth century. No record
exists that shows any explorers or traders who encountered
them east of the Missouri, so their migration westward must
have occurred before the arrival of these European adventurers
in the late seventeenth and early eighteenth centuries. The
Arapaho language belongs to the *Algonquian* family. Because
tribes speaking other languages from this group lived from the
Atlantic coastline westward to the Great Lakes area, it seems
likely that the Arapahos once lived northeast of the Missouri
River and then moved westward onto the plains.

Archaeologists have not been able to conclusively identify any ancient site or *artifact* as belonging to the Arapahos. The tribe's *oral traditions*, however, indicate that they once hunted buffalo on foot. Until about 1730 they probably relied on dogs to help transport their belongings as they followed the immense buffalo herds, moving according to the animals' seasonal migration patterns. Their possessions were often transported on a *travois*, an A-shaped platform whose back end dragged along the ground as it was pulled by a harnessed dog.

Shortly after 1730 the Arapahos seem to have acquired horses by trading with, or raiding, tribes to the south. These people in turn had obtained their horses by raiding Spanish settlements in what is now New Mexico and Texas. The introduction of the horse radically changed the Arapahos' lives. In past years, the Arapahos had driven the buffalo over cliffs or into enclosures, then killed the trapped animals with arrows and spears tipped with stone points, and butchered them with blades of stone or bone. Now hunters mounted on horseback could race alongside the buffalo, killing more efficiently than they had been able to do on foot. The horse also expanded the Arapahos' ability to trade products of the hunt, as well as horses, with other tribes.[4]

The Arapahos had an active trade relationship with the farming villages of the Arikaras, Mandans, and Hidatsas on the Missouri River, exchanging their surplus meat and hides for the villagers' extra beans, corn, and squash. The Arapahos probably acquired not only corn and other agricultural products from these neighboring tribes but new ceremonies as well. The elaborate men's society rituals, and probably other elements of late-eighteenth- and nineteenth-century Arapaho religious life, may have been adapted from or influenced by contacts with these villagers. It was at a trade fair (a gathering of Indian traders and sometimes non-Indian traders as well) in 1795, in the Black Hills of what is now South Dakota, that Arapaho *bands* from the central and southern plains encountered the trader-explorer

Jean Baptiste Trudeau from St. Louis. He left the first written account of the Arapahos. The Arapahos also tried to establish regular trading relations with Taos and, in 1805, several chiefs made a peace and trade agreement with the governor of Santa Fe. In subsequent years, Arapahos traded with Spaniards who came from Taos and elsewhere but also fought with them when the Spanish took Arapaho captives as slaves.[5]

The northern bands of Arapahos, known as the Fall Indians, or *Gros Ventre* ("Big Bellies"), met French-Canadian and English traders in the late eighteenth century in the upper Saskatchewan River country of Canada. Other tribes eventually pushed the Gros Ventres south into Montana, and by the mid-nineteenth century they were living between the Missouri and Milk rivers. In 1878, they settled on a *reservation* in northern Montana, and their history took a course different from that of the Northern or Southern Arapahos, who are the subjects of this book.[6]

In the late eighteenth century, Arapaho bands on the central and southern plains ranged from what is now southeastern Montana and eastern Wyoming south to the headwaters of the Platte River. Pressed by hostile Sioux tribes, who had moved into the Black Hills area, they began to move southwest. By the early nineteenth century the Arapahos controlled the area known as the Parks and adjacent plains in what is now west-central Colorado, and were warring with several neighboring tribes there: the Utes to the west, the Crows north of the Platte River, and the Pawnees to the east. They also were trading with the Kiowas and Comanches to the south in order to increase their supply of horses.

When Trudeau met them they were friendly with the Cheyennes who had recently reached the Missouri and were helping them negotiate with traders. About 1820 the Arapahos and Cheyennes formed a loose alliance and sometimes joined forces in occasional conflicts with the Sioux north of the Platte River and the Kiowas and Comanches to the south. The two allies pushed the Kiowas and Comanches south of the Arkansas River and gradually came to dominate the area between the Platte and Arkansas rivers as far west as present-day eastern Colorado.

In the early nineteenth century, the Arapahos frequently came in contact with American fur trappers and traders in the foothills of the Rocky Mountains and near the headwaters of the Platte and Arkansas rivers. During this time, the Crow language was the trade language used by all the tribes on the southern plains, as well as by Americans. The traders referred to them by the Crow Indians' name for the tribe, *Alappahó*, that is, Arapaho. In sign language, Arapahos were identified as Tattooed People. Arapaho men commonly had three small circles tattooed horizontally across their chests. Women had a single circle tattooed upon their foreheads. The tattoos were made by pricking the skin with cactus spines and rubbing powdered charcoal into the wound. This left a sky-blue mark after healing. In their own language, Arapahos referred to themselves by a term meaning "the people."[7]

The Arapahos sometimes raided trade caravans traveling to and from the Spanish settlement at Santa Fe, but they also traded peacefully with several Americans. These included the brothers William and Charles Bent, who built posts in Arapaho country in the early 1830s. During the first half of the century, the Arapahos continued to hunt. At the same time, they began to incorporate into their tool kits and decorative arts manufactured goods, such as knives and beads, that they acquired from traders.

The Arapahos would become well known to these traders and to the pioneers who crossed the western plains on their way to settle in Oregon and California after 1840. This flood of immigrants would soon ravage the Arapahos' hunting grounds, and the tribe would become increasingly dependent on traders for sustenance, as well as luxury items. Later in the nineteenth century, the U.S. Army would find the Arapahos to be deadly adversaries. Yet, for the most part, the tribe's leaders strove to follow a course of peaceful coexistence with this new and over-whelming civilization. Over many years, traders, military and U.S. government officials, missionaries, journalists, and anthropologists would write about these and other aspects of Arapaho life, as the tribe attempted to defend itself against the onslaught of U.S. expansion.

Until the great disruptions of the 1840s and later, the Arapahos were able to obtain all the necessities of life by hunting big game and gathering roots and berries that existed wild on the prairie. Flat Pipe rituals were held at the start of every spring and fall to ensure the renewal of these seasonal resources. In the spring, the buffalo began to move about in small herds. Arapaho family groups that had been scattered during the winter in the sheltered Rocky Mountain foothills joined forces so the men could hunt buffalo together. Mounted on horses, the men chased the herds. Sometimes they singled out the animals they wanted and cut them off from the rest of the herd in order to kill them more easily. When there were enough men, they would surround the herd and close it in, repeatedly shooting arrows into it until several animals were killed or seriously wounded. Allowing the surviving buffalo to escape, the hunters could finish off those whose wounds forced them to lag behind. Arapaho bows were made of wood—often cedar—supported by layers of sinew (animal tendon) to add flexibility and strength. The arrow points were made of flint. (Later, these were gradu-ally replaced with metal ones as the Arapahos came to trade reg-ularly with the Mexicans and Americans.)

The men butchered the game before bringing it back to camp. They used knives made either of flint or from the shoul-der blade of a buffalo. (Later, they would use metal knives obtained in trade.) After butchering, the meat was transported to camp on the backs of packhorses to be smoked and dried. The women in each family cooked and preserved the meat the hunters brought back and prepared the hides for use as cloth-ing and as tepee covers. In the summer and early fall, when the buffalo herds were largest, the bands regularly came together. They pitched their tepees in a circle. Ceremonies were held in the center of the camp circle, after which groups of men went out to hunt or to raid other tribes, while women worked to dry enough meat, roots, and berries for the winter months.

In winter, the large camps were dissolved again. Each band, composed of twenty to eighty families, moved to its favorite winter campsite in the sheltered, wooded areas along the mountain streams. During this season, the men hunted for deer and small game. They wore snowshoes made of thongs or narrow strips of rawhide forming a net that was fastened to a wooden frame. It was common for a man to use a wood or bone whistle to lure a deer; hunters were expert at imitating the sounds of various animals.

Throughout the year, women's work was as valued as the men's hunting duties. Their work was hard, but women did not consider it drudgery. They were responsible for setting up and moving camp, collecting firewood and edible plants, cooking, and making the family's clothing and shelter. The preparation of animal hides occupied much of the women's time. Rawhide was made by scraping the flesh and hair from a hide, then stretching the skin on the ground, where it was held in position with pegs and left to dry until stiff. Deer or elk skins were used for shirts, dresses, moccasins, and leggings. The skins were soaked, scraped, softened, stretched, and tanned. Then they were cut into the desired pattern and sewn together with sinew pulled through holes punched with an awl.

Women wore dresses that hung almost to the ankle, moccasins with attached leggings that reached the knee and were tied with garters, and, in winter, blankets. Men wore buckskin shirts, leggings that covered their legs from ankle to hip, *breechcloths*, moccasins, and, in winter, robes of buffalo skin. Buffalo hides were thicker than those of deer and elk and were therefore used for robes, as well as tepee covers. Buffalo hair was thickest in the fall, so that is when the women made the

Each Arapaho family had its own tepee, which was made from buffalo hides that were sewn together and wrapped around a circular foundation of poles. This photo is from an Arapaho camp at Fort Sill, Oklahoma, in the early 1870s.

unscraped winter robes. Scraped buffalo skins were used for tepee covers.

A family consisted of a man and his wife or wives (the Arapahos were polygynous), their children, and perhaps other relatives, such as a husband's younger brother or a spouse's widowed parent. Each family had its own tepee. Some tepees were larger than others and had more and better furnishings. These belonged to those men who owned the most horses. They could use more horses to drag extra poles, could accumulate more hides, and could also afford more than one wife. They could lend horses to others, who were then obligated to support their claims to leadership and status. Horse owners received part of the kill and with this surplus could entertain, pay the expenses of ceremonies, and attract followers.

To make a tepee, a foundation of poles was set into the ground. Over it was stretched a covering made of fifteen to twenty buffalo skins sewn together. The base of this cover was secured to the ground with stones or pegs. In winter, the outside of the cover was banked with three feet of earth to retain warmth. The tepee was lined inside, and on this lining were painted pictures of the husband's war exploits.

In the center of the tepee was a fire, which was created by friction from twirling a drill or striking two stones together over tinder. Wood or dried buffalo dung provided the fuel that kept the fire burning. The chief furnishing of the tepee was a foot-high platform that served as both bed and sofa. It was made of poles and rested on the hard-packed dirt floor (wealthier families sometimes covered the floor with buffalo skins). The platform was covered with a woven mat of willow rods that had one end upraised. Covered with hides for warmth and softness, the bed also served as a couch by day. Pillows were made of buckskin stuffed with buffalo hair.

Food was eaten while seated on a piece of rawhide placed on the floor of the tepee. Small pieces of rawhide served as plates, and there were wooden bowls and spoons made of horn. There were no regularly scheduled mealtimes. People ate when they were hungry or when a hunter returned with meat. A meal might consist of dried meat or pemmican (a mixture of dried meat and berries, blended with tallow). Berries, picked by women in summer, were used in several ways: eaten fresh or dried or made into soup. Tea made from herbs such as mint was a favorite beverage. Most dishes were a kind of stew made from meat and wild roots, such as turnips or potatoes. These foods were cut up and put into a rawhide container into which water had been brought to a boil by dropping red-hot stones into the liquid. By the middle of the nineteenth century, however, most families cooked in a metal pot obtained in trade.[8]

Because the Arapahos were on the move much of the time, containers of all sorts were important to the household, and all were made by the women. From buffalo bladders they made bags for carrying water. After the women made camp, water was stored in baskets made of plant fiber and coated with pitch. Women made many types of soft-skin bags for their personal use: pouches to hold quills and paints; sheaths for knives and awls; toilet pouches for face paints, earrings, bracelets, hair parters, and porcupine-tail hairbrushes; and bags for sewing gear. They made large soft-skin bags to carry the household's clothing. They made firmer bags of untanned rawhide, called *parfleches*, which were made in many sizes and used to transport household articles and foodstuffs.

The women painted designs on the stiff rawhide parfleches and embroidered the soft-skin bags. Women also embroidered designs on buckskin tepee ornaments, clothing, and other household objects, incorporating either dyed porcupine quills or, by the mid-nineteenth century, glass beads obtained from traders. Their designs expressed prayers or instructions received in dreams. These designs on robes, cradles, and tepee ornaments were created by women who were considered authorities on ritual matters.[9]

Ritual, prayer, sacrifice, and other signs of religious devotion permeated all aspects of Arapaho life. The Arapahos' decorative art was shaped by prayers and visions; their quest for subsistence was guided by ceremonial acts. From birth to death, concern about relating to the Creator shaped every Arapahos' everyday life. No wonder, then, that the Arapahos, more than any other Plains people he visited, impressed anthropologist James Mooney as "devotees and prophets."

2

The Four Hills of Life

All Arapahos traveled through four stages, or "hills of life": childhood, youth, adulthood, and old age. The duties, responsibilities, and privileges of males and females changed at each stage. The Arapahos symbolically equated the life cycle with the movement of the sun, the four cardinal directions, and the progress of the seasons. They believed, too, that an individual could be reborn after death. A child born with wrinkles or scars and dents, for example, might be the reincarnation of an elder or someone who had suffered wounds in a previous life.

The Arapahos believed that the Creator endowed humans with the ability to think and that thought itself could cause things to happen. Speaking of prenatal life or birth, for example, could cause pregnancy, and people with exceptional powers of thought could cause sterility. If a pregnant woman was startled or badly frightened,

Arapahos traveled through four stages of life: childhood, youth, adulthood, and old age. During childhood, children learned adult tasks through such activities as playing house, participating in games of skill and chance, and mock war games.

the impression left in her mind could cause her child to have birth defects or marks.

Immediately after birth, a baby was rubbed with red paint made of red earth mixed with tallow. The paint symbolized prayers for strength and health. Then the baby was placed inside a cradle made of ornamented buckskin stretched over a willow frame. Dried and finely ground buffalo manure was packed inside the cradle to absorb body wastes and prevent chafing. While the mother worked, she leaned the cradle against a tree, and when she traveled on horseback she attached it to her saddle horn.

When infants were taken out of their cradles, they were wrapped in the tanned hide of an unborn buffalo, with its soft, warm, hairy side against the baby's body. In cold weather, the baby might be put into a bag made from the skin of a wildcat. The baby's head was fitted into the head of the skin and its arms and legs placed into the skin's legs. A baby starting to crawl would be dressed in a tanned deer-hide shirt, and at the toddling stage in adult-style clothing.[10]

Parents took special precautions to protect their children. They arranged for elders to pray on the child's behalf. Because negative wish-thoughts might come true, people refrained from talking about sickness. Symbols of positive wish-thoughts decorated the objects surrounding the child. The baby's cradle was decorated with quillwork designs that represented the maker's prayer for the child to have a long and successful life. Only older women who had the ritual authority to do so could create these designs. At birth, the infant's umbilical cord was cut. It was then put into a beaded case, whose shape represented growth and whose design symbolized the maker's prayer that the child have a long, healthy, and productive life. The case containing the umbilical cord was attached first to the infant's cradle. Later, when the child began to walk, it was attached to his or her clothing.[11]

The child was named by an elder soon after birth. Often the child's parents would invite several elders to a feast at which the name was given, and the elders would pray for the child. A name might be derived from a brave or charitable deed. For example, an old warrior who had been the first to kill an enemy in a particular battle might name a child First Killer. Or a name might come from an extraordinary event or an unusual occurrence in nature—Yellow Bear or White Hawk, for example. An elder might also name a child after something seen in a dream or vision and regarded as a good omen. Elders' prayers were regarded as particularly beneficial because the Creator had blessed elders by allowing them to live long. Thus, if an elder gave a child his or her name, that name was believed to assure good health and a long life for its new recipient as well. Conversely, the name of a child who became ill would often be changed.

To mark special events in the development of a child—when the child first walked or spoke, for example—parents would invite tribal elders to a feast. When a small boy killed his first animal, his parents would invite elders to a feast, announce his feat, and give gifts to the guests in his honor. On all these occasions, the elders would pray for the child.

Parents also arranged for their child's ears to be pierced by a respected old warrior or an old woman who had "pierced" an enemy. Both boys and girls had their ears pierced, usually between the ages of two and five. An awl or a knife was used. The awl symbolized a spear; the hole, the enemy's wound; and the ear ornaments, dripping blood. During the piercing a war song was sung, the piercer told the story of how he had wounded an enemy, and then the piercer "charged" at the child's ear, as he had charged at the enemy. The child's ears also could be pierced during an important religious ceremony such as the *Sun Dance*. In this case, it would be done by an elderly priest, or director, of the ceremony. The piercing here symbolized being struck by lightning—so the child was thereafter protected against enemy arrows. The child's crying was regarded as a sign that hardship and pain, having been endured in the piercing, would not prevent the child from growing up. The ear-piercing ceremony was, in effect, another prayer for a long and successful life.[12]

Children learned adult tasks in play activity, in playing house, and in games of skill and chance. In play, they imitated the activities of their elders. The girls played with toys such as miniature saddlebags, little spoons made of horn, and tepees that were two to three feet high and held beds made with squirrel skins instead of buffalo hides. They also played with dolls made of stuffed buckskin. The dolls were sexless—clothed only in a nondescript buckskin or cloth blanket—and did not represent babies, for speaking of babies was believed to cause pregnancy. Little boys would pretend to hunt for little girls (who pretended to be their mothers) and go to war using horses and enemies made from clay.

Physical activities and sports became more important as a child grew. Children were given ponies and began to ride when they were about three years old. They also became good swimmers, playing games in the creeks and rivers. They might challenge one another as to who could swim under water the farthest and longest; or they might attempt swimming across a river on their backs, with one foot sticking out of the water and a ball of mud impaled on the big toe. Boys competed against one another in shooting arrows, tossing hoops, throwing a javelin, spinning tops, and sliding sticks across the ice. Girls played dice and stick darts and juggled a hair-stuffed buckskin ball on a string, on the foot, or from arm to palm.

Sometimes parents invited an elder who had made a success of his or her life to eat with the family, recount his or her experiences, and advise the child. Grandparents also told the children stories at night—tales of Trickster, or Spider, the wonder-worker. These stories conveyed the values by which the Arapahos lived, for Trickster was always undone by his foolish behavior.[13]

When boys and girls reached about twelve years of age, their training for adult life began in earnest. Boys and girls were separated from one another, and even brothers and sisters now had to avoid talking to one another or even being in the other's presence.

When Arapaho boys and girls reached the age of twelve, their training for adult life began. Once girls reached puberty, their freedom was restricted. They spent most of their time with their mothers or other female relatives, who would prepare them for adulthood by teaching them how to cook, tan skins, and make clothing.

Unlike some other tribes, the Arapahos held no ceremony for a girl when she had her first menstrual period, nor was she isolated in a special tepee. However, because menstruation was believed tinged with a supernatural power that might harm others in certain circumstances, the girls stayed apart from the rest of the tribe. They kept company mostly with old women and avoided sacred ceremonies. After puberty there were restrictions on a young woman's freedom. She might wear a blanket to conceal her figure, and her dresses were now long sleeved and hung almost to the ankle, like those of older women. She would often live with a grandmother or other elderly female relative, who would teach her how to prepare food, tan skins, and make clothing.

Young girls and adult women spent considerable time on their appearance. In the early part of the nineteenth century, women wore their hair loose and painted it. Later, they parted the hair from forehead to nape and made two braids from behind the ear. They used sweet-smelling leaves and seeds to perfume their clothing and hair. The face was painted daily to protect it from the elements.

Teenage boys, meanwhile, were instructed by older male relatives on how to hunt, make a living, and develop those social traits the Arapahos admired. During their early teens, they were encouraged to participate in the Kit Fox ceremony. The Kit Fox was the first of the societies that Arapaho boys and men belonged to in the course of their lives. Young teenage boys would band together and persuade a man about ten years older to act as their adviser. Under his tutelage, they prepared for the ceremony by learning the Kit Fox dance and songs. After completing the ceremony, they were bound together, obligated to assist and support one another for the rest of their lives. As Kit Foxes they trained together for adult life, racing on foot and horseback, wrestling, engaging in mock battles, and raiding households to steal meat from drying racks. They might also be sent by their families on errands that required them to travel alone across the prairie to another camp as many as thirty miles away.[14]

When they reached their late teens, Kit Foxes moved on to join the Stars. With the counsel of this group's older advisers, the boys learned the Star Dance and the associated songs in preparation for the Star ceremony. The ceremony strengthened the bond among the group's members. As Starmen, they would have more responsibilities in camp life. Membership in the Stars prepared them for entry into the four sacred lodges to which Arapaho men belonged.

When a young man reached his twenties, he was allowed to go on his first buffalo hunt. He first invited several old men to a feast, where they instructed him and made his arrows, painting them with markings to identify their owner. The young hunter was told to give his first kill to an old man, who would pray for him. He might also be allowed by his elders to go into the hills to fast and pray, as part of what was called a *vision quest*—a search for a vision in which supernatural beings would promise special guidance. If he had such an experience, he was required to confide this to an old man who supervised his spiritual development. During the course of several vision quests, a young man received instructions from the supernatural helper about either warfare or curing. The old man helped to interpret these instructions.

Before a man could marry, he had to show that he could support a wife and family. For this reason most men married when they were about thirty years old, by which time they might have achieved military success, acquired horses by raiding other tribes, and gained the means to provide for their families. Young women, however, usually married in their late teens.

Although young women were discouraged from being near young men and were watched closely to prevent such contacts, they sometimes managed secret meetings. A young man might try to get the attention of a young woman by flashing a mirror or playing a flute outside her tepee. Or he might, while standing outside the tepee, take the poles that controlled the smoke flaps and move them so as to cause the tepee to fill with smoke. Then, if the young woman's father or grandfather asked her to go outside to adjust the poles, the suitor would have a chance to talk with her briefly. A young man might also meet a young woman when she was sent to fetch water or go on another errand, or when she visited one of his own female relatives.

Most marriages, however, were arranged by a young woman's older brother, father, or uncle. Her male relatives would choose a man they believed would be a good provider; often he was a friend of the brother. If a man admired a particular young woman, he might speak to her brother himself or send his female relatives to ask her family for consent to the marriage. If a young woman disliked a man who was selected for her, she could refuse to marry him. This seldom happened, however, because her relatives invariably pressured her to agree to the family's wishes. No relatives could be considered as prospective husbands or wives; the Arapahos considered their uncles and aunts to be as close in relationship as their own parents. In fact, the same term was used to describe a person's father and paternal uncle (father's brother). Similarly, a person's maternal aunts (mother's sisters) were referred to by the same term as the mother. There was no word for cousin—all the children of one's parents' brothers and sisters were considered the same as one's own brothers and sisters. Even people whose relationship was what we call second and third cousins were considered too closely related to marry.

An elderly Arapaho woman who was married in about 1868 told ethnologist Truman Michelson in 1932 how her marriage came about:

> Since I was not acquainted with the young man who became my husband, he sent his mother, two of his own sisters, and his paternal aunt to ask my brother and my maternal uncles for permission to marry me. My brother had given his consent before I was aware of it, as I happened to be away at the time. When I came to our tepee my brother came to me, which was unusual, sat near me and started to tell me what he had done, and that he had done so for the good of our

father and mother. My father had expressed his willingness also. So when my mother started to talk to me, asking me to say what I thought, I told her that if my brother said it was all right, it would be all right with me, as I didn't want to hurt his feelings by refusing.[15]

Another elderly woman, telling her girlhood experiences to anthropologist Inez Hilger in 1936, said that when her uncle arranged for her marriage against her wishes, she at first ran away:

> It was almost sundown. . . . I pulled my shawl over my head and face and cried, but kept on running. . . . It was getting dark. The owls were already hooting. I was "wild"! While I was still running, a horse passed me and circled around me. . . . A woman grabbed me, landed me on the horse, and took me back to camp. . . . I still insisted that I wasn't going to be married to him. . . . In the morning my uncles talked to me, and then I was willing to be married.[16]

On the day of the wedding, the groom's family brought horses and other gifts to the bride's family, and the bride's family responded by giving an equivalent amount of property. After this exchange, the bride's family set up a tepee and furnished it, then invited the groom and his family there for a feast. At this feast, the bride and groom sat together publicly for the first time, the marriage was announced, and elders prayed for the couple and instructed them on how to live a proper married life. The two families again exchanged presents, completing the marriage ceremony. Men gave horses and sometimes quivers (a case for carrying arrows), bows and arrows, and saddles. Women gave robes, clothing, and other household goods. Throughout the marriage, a woman retained her own property; she owned horses and the tepee and its furnishings.

Occasionally, when a family did not approve of a match, a couple would elope, much to the disapproval of the girl's family. When the couple returned and set up housekeeping, the husband might send a gift of horses to his wife's family so that the marriage was accepted, even if somewhat begrudgingly.

When a single man married, he hunted for game on behalf of his bride's family, and his mother-in-law cooked for the couple even if they had their own tepee. Only gradually did young women assume their full housekeeping responsibilities. If a man took a second wife, the senior or "boss" wife directed all the work of the household. Many men had two wives, and the most prosperous men had more, but before he took more than one, a man had to be able to provide for his wives and children. Usually a man who had more than one wife would marry a sister of his first wife, assuming that her family had found him to be a good husband. That way the wives would get along well with one another, and the husband's relationship with his in-laws was strengthened.

After marriage, the husband was expected to avoid his mother-in-law, and the wife her father-in-law. If they had to communicate, intermediaries were used. A teasing, joking relationship usually developed between a man and his wife's sisters and between a woman and her husband's brothers. Sometimes a husband's brother would rub soot on his fingers, steal into his sister-in-law's tepee, and blacken her nose and eyebrows while she slept. Brothers-in-law also teased each other. It was a favorite Arapaho joke for one to say the other was bowlegged because his mother had changed the dried manure in his cradle so rarely that it had become wadded like a ball between his knees. The butt of the joke might retort that his bowleggedness came from riding a horse as soon as he was able to walk.[17]

There were four societies, or lodges, to which adult men could belong: the Tomahawk, Spear, Crazy, and Dog lodges. A man who was not initiated into the men's lodges could never be respected or obtain a position of responsibility. After completing the Star ceremony, young men seeking success in war or the restoration of health (whether their own or that of others) could vow to sponsor the next and more sacred ceremony of the Tomahawk Lodge. They were probably in their middle or late twenties when they did so. A vow to sponsor or the decision to participate in a lodge ceremony was considered a form of sacrificial prayer.

A young man who wanted to sponsor the Tomahawk Lodge ceremony would petition an older man (probably a Spearman in his thirties) to advise him and his fellow Starmen. Each candidate would seek out an older man, referred to as a "Grandfather," who had completed the Tomahawk Lodge, and ask for instruction in the sacred songs and regalia. The Tomahawk Lodge ceremony, like that of the other three men's lodges, lasted for seven days and was held in the summer, when all the Arapahos were camped together. During the first three days, the young men were taught the secrets of the ceremony, and those who had been bravest in battle were chosen by the older men to carry special regalia in the coming dance. This honor recognized the courage of its recipients and at the same time obligated them to do even braver deeds. During the remaining four days, the men danced to the newly learned songs, which were actually prayers to the Creator. The ceremony was believed to confer great strength and potency on the young men. The Grandfather and his chosen grandson not only exchanged gifts but could thereafter never oppose each other. Either one could with propriety prevent the other from committing a violent act against another Arapaho; thus the relationship helped to keep peace in the camp.

As time passed, the young men of the Tomahawk Lodge gained experience in battle and took on increasing responsibilities in the camp. Eventually one would face danger or ill health and vow to sponsor the Spear Lodge—more sacred than the Tomahawk—in return for supernatural aid to get him out of his predicament. His fellow Tomahawkmen again joined him in seeking Grandfathers, this time older men who had completed the Spear Lodge, to instruct them. As before, the first three days of the ceremony were spent in making regalia and learning songs. Again, the bravest men carried distinct regalia. In return, each honoree was expected one day to plant his lance in the earth during a battle and not retreat from it until it was removed by a fellow warrior. The Spear Lodge ceremony was considered to bestow overall success but especially supernatural aid in battle. In addition to serving as warriors, the Spearmen took on new responsibilities for keeping order in the camp and on the hunt and protecting their people when traveling across the open prairie. Most men married at about the time they entered the Spear Lodge.

Men who were about forty years of age were considered mature enough to vow the Crazy Lodge. This lodge was more sacred than the Spear Lodge, and a man normally decided to vow it when he found himself in need of supernatural aid. The vower and his fellow Spearmen would again choose Grandfathers who had already completed the Crazy ceremony. As before, the first three days of the ceremony were devoted to learning the songs and making the regalia of the dance that followed. The Crazymen carried small bows and arrows during the dance, and in the ceremony they were taught how to use the extract of a particular root on their arrows to paralyze animals and humans in the hunt or times of war. They also learned how to walk on hot coals and how to use a particular root to prevent fatigue. After pledging the Crazy Lodge, men had ceremonial duties; for example, they assisted younger warriors' efforts to be successful in battle. The wives of candidates for the Crazy Lodge also participated in the ceremony of transfer, for the Crazy Lodge symbolically expressed the idea that life had male and female components, each necessary to the other.

When men reached their late forties or early fifties, it became appropriate to vow the Dog Lodge, the next and more sacred lodge in the series. Men who completed this ceremony directed battles and helped inspire younger warriors to brave deeds. Most leaders of the Arapaho bands were Dogmen. They and their wives acquired particularly great powers from their

Adult Arapaho men progressively joined four ceremonial organizations: the Tomahawk, Spear, Crazy, and Dog lodges. Shown here are figures that represent an officer of the Dog society (left) and a member of the Crazy society. Men usually entered the Crazy Lodge when they were approximately forty years old. Following the Crazy Lodge, Arapaho men usually entered the Dog Lodge in their late forties or early fifties, at which time they had generally risen to the status of military leader. These lodges had governmental duties, as well as religious purposes.

Grandfathers in this lodge—speed in battle, protection from bullets, and the ability to live into old age. At the age of about sixty, Dogmen were eligible to join the Stoic Lodge of the old men.[18]

Adult men of any age could pledge to sponsor or participate in the Offerings or Sacrifice Lodge, also known as the Sun Dance. This or one of the other men's lodges was held every summer. As required for the other lodges, a man needed a Grandfather for the *Offerings Lodge*. During the first three days of this ceremony, the pledger was instructed in secret by elder ritual authorities. For the next four days, the rest of the participants received instructions from their Grandfathers, fasted, and danced to exhaustion. The fasting and dancing were aspects of sacrifice. Another type of sacrifice was self-torture. A man tied one end of a thong to the lodge's center pole, hooked the other end into his chest, and pulled away from the pole until his flesh tore. This was considered sacrificing a piece of flesh. The Sacrifice Lodge was the most respected of the prayer-sacrifice rites because it called for both immense physical suffering and large donations of property on the part of the dancers and their families. The Sacrifice Lodge symbolically expressed events in Arapaho mythology. It was believed to assist the physical and spiritual well-being of all Arapahos, and its successful completion required harmony and cooperation. Each time a man participated in a ceremony, he gained ritual knowledge, prestige, and authority. He could serve as Grandfather to a younger man or direct some phase of that ceremony.[19]

A man might also obtain supernatural power for his personal use by petitioning the Creator for contact with a supernatural being. The degree and kind of power characteristic of each type of supernatural being varied, but the Creator's agents could confer the ability to cure sickness, to assure success in war and other ventures, to control the weather, and to foretell the future. A man seeking supernatural power fasted alone on a hill or mountain peak, concentrating his thoughts and making offerings over a period of one to seven days. If he were successful, a supernatural being came to him, usually in the form of an animal that changed into human form and gave him specific powers. The seeker also received instructions in how to use his power, a song associated with the power, and an object or objects that symbolized or served as a vehicle of the power. Some men had dreams in which supernatural beings appeared, without having been sought, and offered them power. Sometimes a man refused power, for it had the potential to harm the recipient or his relatives if misused. Power was supposed to be used only for good; sorcery, the use of supernatural power for evil purposes, could cause harm to its owner, as well as to intended victims. A man carried his power objects in a medicine bag and sometimes painted images from his vision on his tepee, or, if his power was for war, on his shield. He might also wear power objects, such as feathers. A man could give or sell his supernatural power to another person, along with the instructions for its use and the medicine bag objects that were associated with it.[20]

In warfare men sought to do brave deeds. This might involve killing an enemy in a way that brought personal risk. Rushing into the fray and striking an enemy, stealing horses from inside an enemy camp, and taking a scalp or other war trophy from an enemy also involved risk, and these deeds were as esteemed as killing an enemy, if not more so. Performing any of these activities entitled a man to take a new name commemorating his deed and to paint his exploits on his tepee lining or his shirt.

Men wore their hair in a way that symbolized their bravery in war. Early in the nineteenth century, they wore their hair parted on each side and standing upright in the center over the forehead. Over their temples, their hair was cut into a zigzag edge. In front of their ears the hair hung down, either braided or tied together. They thought that wearing the hair upright over the forehead made them look fierce. Later, men braided the hair or tied it in masses over their ears and kept a scalp lock in the center at the back of their head. They tied feathers or other objects symbolic of their supernatural helpers onto the hair.

Performing brave deeds helped a man build a reputation and gain prestige. For example, acquiring a large number of horses through raiding enabled a man not only to support a large household but also to be generous to others, and public generosity was requisite to leadership. If a man donated to ceremonies and gave generously to elders, widows, and orphans and if he was even-tempered and competent, he might be selected by other men and elders to become the leader of his band.

Decisions for the camp as a whole were generally made by consensus among the adult men and some of the elderly women. Elderly ritual authorities and the leaders of the men's lodges were particularly influential. It was the band leader's job to gain a consensus and then to persuade others to abide by that consensus. He and the other influential men could rely on the men of the lodges to enforce decisions if necessary. A lodge could, for example, destroy a man's personal belongings and even kill his horse for violating the rules of a hunt.

Elder women, like elder men, had authority in religious matters, and older women had considerable influence over family affairs. At every age, a woman could help her husband improve his position and at the same time gain prestige for herself and her children in a number of ways. She could make prayer-sacrifices of property; wives often gave away their own property generously to others on behalf of their husbands (and sometimes brothers). She could vow to sponsor or participate in the women's sacred Buffalo Lodge, which was believed to help ensure success in the buffalo hunt. She could also offer physical suffering on behalf of family members.

One woman told anthropologist Truman Michelson of the circumstances behind her own sacrifice. When her sister became ill and two of the best Arapaho doctors failed to cure her, she explained:

> I unhesitatingly made a vow to sacrifice my left little finger, so that my sister's life might be spared, so that her small children, who were a pitiful sight to me as they were about their helpless mother, might again enjoy happiness. . . . The next morning an Arapaho woman was called to remove my finger in the usual way. . . . My sister commenced to get better, improving very quickly.[21]

Women made designs using quills and beads that served as prayers for the well-being of their owner on garments and other household objects. When they made moccasins, for example, they would often work prayers in symbolic form into the design.

Women also could acquire through dreams the individually owned supernatural power to use herbs for healing; in the dreams they were shown what plants to use and how to use them. A man could give his individually owned supernatural power to his wife. Women made essential contributions to all of the tribal ceremonies by preparing the food considered essential to the establishment and maintenance of relationships between Grandfather and Grandson, priest and devotee, and humans and the Creator.

Maintaining the Arapahos' good standing with the Creator was primarily the responsibility of old people, particularly the elderly ritual authorities. Most prominent among these were the Stoic Lodge members, the seven Water-Pouring Old Men, and the keeper of the Flat Pipe bundle.

Men of sixty or so completed the Stoic Lodge. This ceremony involved four nights of fasting and prayer led by seven tribal priests called Water-Pouring Old Men and was so sacred that young people did not go near it. The Stoicmen had the responsibility of praying for the well-being of all Arapahos and were supposed to think only good thoughts. "Whatever they prayed for was thought to be granted," one Arapaho told anthropologist Inez Hilger.[22]

The Stoicmen had the right and duty to paint the people with sacred red paint, which in a variety of ways promoted or restored health or a sense of well-being. They painted the faces of mourners, for example, to reintegrate them into the society after the period of mourning was over. Just as the newborn baby was painted with the red sacred paint, the body, face, and hair of a dead person were painted before burial. Elders applied red paint to their own faces daily. The paint symbolized old age, sacredness, and earth or subsistence; thus the very appearance of the aged reminded other Arapahos of the elders' central role in the tribe's well-being.

The seven Water-Pouring Old Men also directed all the lodge ceremonies. These elderly ritual leaders wore their hair uncombed and gathered in a bunch over the forehead. Every day when the tribe was camped together, they prayed in a large domed lodge, called a sweat lodge, in the center of the camp circle. Inside the sweat lodge, they poured water over hot coals to make steam, which helped their prayers ascend to the Creator. Each Water-Pouring Old Man was custodian of a bag containing a rattle and sacred paint. The rattle was used in prayer-songs and the paint in all religious ceremonies. Symbolically, these seven men represented the former custodians of the Flat Pipe bundle, central to the Arapaho creation myth, and they were responsible for helping to conduct ceremonies involving the Flat Pipe.

The Flat Pipe bundle itself was in the custody of an old man known as the keeper. He represented the First Pipe Keeper, the mythological being who had been given the Pipe on behalf of the Arapahos, and was himself regarded as sacred. The keeper conducted rites to ensure the annual renewal of the earth and the continued prosperity of the tribe. He used his authority to generate consensus and resolve conflict.

The Flat Pipe bundle was referred to as "Old Man" and kept in a special tepee, painted with sacred designs, that stood in the center of the camp circle. In addition to the Pipe, the bundle contained other objects that represented events in the creation story. It was suspended on a stand of four sticks. Proper care of the Flat Pipe was necessary to maintain a harmonious relationship with the Creator and nature. If the Pipe were destroyed, an earthquake or flood would follow. Arapahos who wished to make prayers to the Creator through the Flat Pipe could accompany their prayers with a sacrifice of property, usually robes. Later, the keeper distributed these offerings to the needy.

Like the seven tribal bags kept by the Water-Pouring Old Men, there were seven sacred bags kept by seven old women. These bags held incense and implements for painting and quill embroidery. The seven women attained their positions by fasting and other kinds of sacrifice. Using the sacred objects in their bags, they supervised the embroidery of tepee ornaments and the decoration of buffalo robes and cradles. They prayed that the designs, which represented prayers for health and long life, would be executed correctly and accomplish the desired ends. Men were excluded from these rites.[23]

Old people, both male and female, had extensive authority not only in ceremonies but in the daily lives of children, youths, and mature adults. They gave frequent orations praising noteworthy individuals and supporting the actions of tribal leaders. Younger Arapahos usually followed their elders' wishes, and relied constantly on their knowledge and prayers, believing that elders were most qualified to mediate between the people and the Creator.

In the mid-nineteenth century, however, the spiritual beliefs of the Arapahos, as well as their way of life, would come under assault as intruders entered their territory and altered forever the world as the Arapahos knew it.

3

The Struggle to Survive

Before 1841, the Arapahos depended on hunting buffalo to provide the basis of their subsistence. By hunting small game and collecting edible plant foods they rounded out their diet. From plant and animal materials available in their environment, they made almost everything else they needed. Since the early nineteenth century, they had been in contact with traders, to whom they gave horses and buffalo robes in exchange for manufactured goods, which were luxuries for them. Arapaho women prized red, white, and blue glass beads, woolen trade cloth, metal cooking pots, brass wire for bracelets, and Navajo blankets. Arapaho men sought metal knives, tobacco, iron for arrowheads, and, above all, guns and ammunition to defend themselves against enemy tribes to the east that already possessed firearms.

In the 1840s, emigrants from the eastern United States began traveling westward through Arapaho country on their way to what are now the states of Oregon, California, and Utah. At first they followed the Oregon Trail along the North Platte River, through what is now Wyoming, to Sweetwater River and into Utah. In

Bent's Fort

Traders working out of St. Louis, Missouri, came to Arapaho country in the early nineteenth century to trap or trade beaver pelts. In Europe and the United States, there was a great demand for men's hats made of beaver felt, and trading companies competed with each other for these furs. Charles Bent was born in 1799 and worked for the Missouri Fur Company in the 1820s. He was drawn to the upper Arkansas River area because of the opportunities to obtain beaver and because Santa Fe had become a prominent trading town. There, goods produced in Spanish settlements could be obtained and transported back to the Missouri River. Similarly, Santa Fe was a market for goods shipped from St. Louis. Charles's younger brother, William, born in 1809, joined him in his trading ventures on the Arkansas River in eastern Colorado in the late 1820s.

William used the Arkansas River as a means to travel to Indian villages in order to trade. During his travels, he met a band of Cheyennes who had migrated to the area of the Arkansas River from the Cheyenne River in South Dakota and became friends with the leader of this group, the Hairy Ropes. He and his brother Charles also became partners with Ceran St. Vrain, who had been trading in Santa Fe—the group transported goods between Santa Fe and St. Louis and traded with Indians for buffalo robes. By about 1830, the market for beaver had collapsed because silk hats had begun to become popular, but the market for buffalo robes was beginning to expand in the eastern United States. To better take advantage of trade with various Native tribes, the partners decided to build a fort on the Arkansas, where Indians could bring their robes. Employees could travel from the fort to Indian camps, acquire robes, return to the fort for supplies, and start the process over again.

Bent's Fort was built near the mouth of the Purgatoire River on the Arkansas and was larger than a modern football field. Its walls were three feet thick, and it was protected by cannons. Inside on the ground level were

1848, the United States successfully concluded a two-year war against Mexico to expand its southwestern frontier. As a result, travel on the Santa Fe Trail increased dramatically after 1848, as

warehouses for goods, a kitchen and dining hall, blacksmith shop, tailor and carpenter workshops, and an area for Indian customers, which was separated by a barrier from the storerooms. There was a large corral with cactus planted on the top to prevent thieves from getting inside to remove stock. The fort had a fleet of wagons and a press where buffalo robes were compressed before they were packed for shipping. A second story area offered more living space and the fort housed about two hundred people and four hundred animals. The construction was largely completed by 1833 and a trading license was issued by the federal government in 1834.

The fort attracted Indians from several tribes, particularly the Arapahos, in whose homeland the fort was built, and Cheyenne groups who gradually migrated into the area to join the Hairy Ropes. William Bent forged a special relationship with the Cheyennes. He married Owl Woman and Yellow Woman, the daughters of the Cheyennes' religious leader. In exchange for their robes and moccasins, the Indians received cloth, Navajo blankets, knives, beads, mirrors, gun powder and lead, guns, and hard bread. In the winter, when the buffalos' hides were in prime condition, traders went out from the post to the Indian camps. The traders would be taken into the camp leader's tepee, where the leader could protect him and supervise the trade. There was reciprocal gift-giving and feasting before the trading began. Charles Bent secured presidential medals from the federal government and presented these prized symbols of leadership to Arapaho and Cheyenne principal chiefs. The Bents tried to stay on good terms with the tribes in the area and successfully competed with other trading interests. Between 1835 and 1839, they built another post on the South Platte River to trade with Arapaho, Cheyenne, and Sioux bands that ranged north of the Arkansas River.*

* Information adapted from David Lavender, *Bent's Fort* (New York: Doubleday and Company, 1954).

travelers streamed westward through what is now Kansas, across the Arkansas River, and southwest to Santa Fe. After the discovery of gold in California in 1848, there was a significant increase in traffic along the Platte River route.

An early result of these intrusions was the disruption of the migratory pattern of the buffalo herds on which the Arapahos depended. Ultimately, the buffalo population declined drastically. Before the nineteenth century came to a close, American westward expansion would threaten the Arapahos' very survival.

Explorer John C. Frémont noted that, in contrast to conditions in 1843, in the 1820s and 1830s large herds of buffalo were never out of a traveler's view from the Rocky Mountains to the Missouri River. Gradually the herds came to occupy more restricted territory, moving into areas away from the lanes of travel. Medicine Man, a representative of the Northern Arapahos in the late 1850s and 1860s, spoke to federal officials about the tribe's plight:

> Our country for hunting game has become very small. We see the white men everywhere. Their rifles kill some of the game, and the smoke of their campfires scares the rest away . . . . It is but a few years ago when we encamped here, in this valley of Deer Creek, and remained many moons, for the buffalo were plenty, and made the prairie look black all around us. Now none are to be seen. . . . Our old people and little children are hungry for many days . . . for our hunters can get no meat. Our sufferings are increasing every winter. Our horses are dying because we ride them so far to get a little game for our lodges. We wish to live.

Despite these provocations, the Arapahos did not attack the wagon trains. As the buffalo became scarce, however, competition escalated among Indian tribes over hunting territory. To defend themselves, the Arapahos, along with their allies the Cheyennes, needed guns and ammunition that could be

The buffalo played an important role in the life of the Arapahos, but by the 1860s, white hunters had greatly reduced the number of buffalo in Arapaho territory. As the buffalo became scarce, the Arapahos became increasingly dependent on Indian agents to supply manufactured goods and food. Shown here is an Arapaho camp in Kansas in which buffalo meat is drying in front of the tepees.

obtained only through trade. They especially desired new rifles such as those possessed by Indians who lived farther east. They quickly recognized that it was not in their best interest to drive away traders and others who had the goods they wanted. Instead, the Arapahos found it more practical to refrain from attacks and extract "presents" from travelers in return for letting them pass through without being molested. Wagon trains along the Arkansas and Platte river routes were confronted with long lines of mounted warriors waving American flags and bearing letters from officials attesting to their good character. The Indians solicited arms, ammunition, and luxuries such as tobacco, sugar, bread, and coffee in return for the safe passage of the wagon trains.

The people on these wagon trains often carried published guidebooks that advised them how to travel safely through the plains. One, entitled the *Parsons Guidebook*, stressed that when travelers reached Arapaho and Cheyenne country, they would encounter Indians desiring supplies. Treat them well, advised the guidebook: if three or four, feed them; if in bands of two or three hundred, feed the chief men.

Several Arapaho leaders developed reputations among the travelers as "friendly chiefs." They would approach the caravans dressed in military uniforms, wearing medals given them by U.S. government officials and carrying documents that introduced them as "friendly." These credentials entitled them to receive gifts and hospitality from the travelers. The friendly chiefs used their privileged status to attract and hold on to the loyalty of their followers. They distributed the gifts they received to their followers. This was in full accord with Arapaho tradition: To be accepted as a leader, to gain prestige, one had to be generous to others. Some of the friendly chiefs, such as Friday of the Northern Arapahos and Left Hand of the Southern Arapahos, became fluent in English, which helped them represent their people to the American travelers and U.S. government officials.

Friday had been named Black Spot at birth. While still a child, he was inadvertently left behind one day in 1831 when his people moved camp. He wandered for days until the trapper and trader Thomas Fitzpatrick found him on the Cimarron River in southeastern Colorado. Fitzpatrick named the boy Friday, for the day on which he found him. The trader became so fond of young Friday that he took him to St. Louis to live with him. He also sent Friday to school for two years, where he learned English. Until 1838, Friday stayed with the trader, traveling west into Indian country with him and becoming accustomed to and learning about the Americans, or "mysterious ones," as the Arapahos called them. On one of these trips west in 1838, they entered a camp of Northern Arapahos, and

Friday, now a young man, was recognized by his relatives. He then rejoined his people, taking his place as a hunter and warrior. One of Fitzpatrick's contemporaries wrote: "Few Indians or whites can compete with Friday as a buffalo-hunter, either in the use of the bow or rifle. I have seen him kill five of these animals at a single chase, and am informed that he has not infrequently exceeded that number."

As a young warrior, Friday began to build a reputation for bravery against the Arapahos' enemies, the Pawnees, Shoshones, and Utes. In one fight with the Utes, he engaged a warrior in hand-to-hand combat, snatched the warrior's loaded gun away when it failed to fire, and then killed him. He and others in the war party destroyed a village of seven tepees that day. Fighting against the Pawnees, he shot a pony out from under a man in the thickest part of the fight.

But Friday's renown among his people came primarily from his skill as an interpreter and intermediary. Comfortable with the Americans, he smoothed over quarrels and misunderstandings, and on more than one occasion prevented attacks on the Arapahos. Friday interpreted for John Frémont and other explorers, and for U.S. Army officers sent to keep peace along the immigration routes in the 1840s. He also served as interpreter to Little Owl, the Northern Arapaho chief, in the 1850s, and to his successor, Medicine Man.

Less is known of Left Hand. He apparently made a trip east of the Missouri in the 1850s, when he was middle-aged, and seems to have received instruction in English before then. In 1859, he was recognized by settlers and U.S. government officials as an important Southern Arapaho leader who visited them frequently and tried to maintain good relations between his people and theirs.

The U.S. government was eager to encourage settlement of the West. Officials were concerned about the hazards posed to Anglo settlers by clashes among various warring tribes and between the Indians and the settlers themselves. In 1846,

Thomas Fitzpatrick was appointed federal Indian *agent* for the Arapahos and other tribes along and between the Platte and Arkansas rivers. Fitzpatrick, who was well respected by the Arapahos, sought their continued goodwill by visiting them and distributing gifts of sugar and coffee. He urged them not to retaliate against the travelers who were damaging their buffalo range. Shortly after becoming agent, Fitzpatrick married Margaret Poisal, the daughter of Left Hand's sister and an American trader. Fitzpatrick's marriage to Left Hand's niece further cemented his relationship with the tribe.

A few years later, his superiors in Washington, D.C., instructed him to arrange a council between representatives of the federal government and of the tribes under his jurisdiction. They hoped to obtain an agreement that the tribes would remain in well-defined areas of occupation in order to minimize conflicts that threatened the safe passage of homesteaders.

The site selected for the treaty council was on Horse Creek, thirty-five miles east of Fort Laramie, Wyoming. On August 31, 1851, the Indians began arriving—ten thousand Arapahos, Cheyennes, Sioux, and a few Crows, Shoshones, and others from north of the Platte River. In all, most of the Plains Indians were represented. The horse herds were so large that in only a few days the grass was stripped away for miles around by their grazing. To the amazement of the U.S. government officials, no fights broke out, even between tribes that routinely battled one another. All had made a sacred pledge to keep the peace. Each tribe put on displays of horsemanship and battle skills. Feasts were held during the day, and dances at night, while the Indian leaders talked to the officials from Washington, D.C.

On September 17, the Indians signed a treaty in which they agreed to curtail war parties, refrain from attacking U.S. citizens, and allow military posts to be built in Indian territory. Each tribe was assigned a particular tract of land as its primary residence, although hunting and traveling outside these tracts were permitted. The Arapahos, along with the Cheyennes, were acknowledged to have control over the area between the North Platte and Arkansas rivers, west to the foothills of the Rocky Mountains. During the council, each tribe chose intermediary chiefs, leaders whom the United States could consider representatives. The Arapahos selected Little Owl, of the Northern Arapahos, to be their primary spokesman; they also selected the Southern Arapaho chiefs Cut Nose and Big Man. The Arapahos expected these leaders to express the wishes of the group as a whole, not to make agreements on their own. In return for their concessions, all of the Indians at the Horse Creek council were promised an annual distribution of blankets, cloth, clothing, metal utensils and tools, and guns and ammunition.

After these intermediary chiefs signed the treaty, presents were distributed. The most important men each received a major general's uniform and a medal; other influential men received similar, though less impressive, gifts. One of the soldiers at the treaty council described a newly bedecked chief:

> Wearing a saber, [and a] medal with the head of the President on one side and clasped hands on the other, he carries a document with an immense seal and ribbon thereon—enclosed in a large envelope, that he may show all comers what the Great Father [the President] thinks of him—what rank and power he wields among his fellow man.

Twenty-seven wagonloads of presents—including tobacco, cloth, paint, blankets, knives, beads, sugar, and coffee—were delivered to the designated chiefs, and each distributed the presents among the people of his tribe. Delegates, Friday among them, were also chosen to go east to meet with President Millard Fillmore. They returned from Washington, D.C., with gifts from the president, including a flag and a medal for each. They also came back with the clear realization that if the Arapahos offered military opposition to western expansion,

Sent to school by Thomas Fitzpatrick, an American trader, Chief Friday was a valuable interpreter for the Northern Arapahos. In the early 1850s, Friday, along with several Arapaho delegates, met with President Millard Fillmore in Washington, D.C. Though they were treated well and presented with many gifts, they understood that resistance to western expansion by the United States was futile and it was in their best interest to ally themselves with the federal government.

they would be destroyed by a larger and more technologically advanced society.

There was another reason why the Arapahos needed to remain on good terms with the Americans. As wild game became more and more scarce, the Indians came to rely increasingly on gifts of manufactured goods. At first such gifts were regarded as luxuries, but by the 1860s they had become necessities. Hunters could no longer find enough buffalo to make clothing and robes to trade for goods. The Arapahos came to depend on the Indian agent, who distributed large quantities of blankets, different kinds of cloth, needles, thread, shirts, shawls, ribbon, beads, vermilion (a red pigment used as paint or dye), and brass wire, as well as a few hats, umbrellas, and handkerchiefs that were sought for their prestige value. Good conduct also brought from the agent a large annual reward of percussion and flintlock rifles. Although the bow and arrow was very efficient for hunting buffalo, these guns were essential for hunting the smaller game upon which the tribe increasingly relied.

The Arapahos' situation became particularly precarious in the 1850s because the heartland of their hunting territory—the western portion of the land designated in 1851 for the Cheyennes and the Arapahos—became flooded with caravans and settlers. In 1856, Americans began to settle permanently in the Smoky Hill River valley, one of the few remaining buffalo ranges. In 1858, prospectors joining the *gold rush* to the Pike's Peak area in Colorado took over the Arapahos' favorite camp-sites along the headwaters of the South Platte River and in the Parks.

Denver and other towns were quickly constructed. Despite the 1851 treaty, which permitted homesteaders only passage through the Indians' land, not permanent occupancy, the federal government made no effort to halt the growth of the towns. The U.S. government counted on the gold from these areas to develop the nation's economy.

The spread of the towns brought about a crucial event in Arapaho history: the splitting of the tribe into two divisions, northern and southern. Before settlements became extensive, bands of Arapahos in the north had roamed what is now Colorado and southern Wyoming, whereas those in the south had ranged between the South Platte and Arkansas rivers. The incursions of miners and homesteaders drove the northern-ranging bands still farther north, whereas those in the south tried to stay below the increasingly crowded Denver area. By 1855, the two divisions were politically self-contained and independent of each other, and each had its own Indian agent assigned by the federal government. Separation was a gradual process, but it ultimately brought about differing identities for the two divisions. The Northern Arapahos formed an alliance with the Sioux and Northern Cheyennes and were able to hunt in what is now Wyoming and Montana, an area that was sparsely populated and hence less threatening to their existence. The Southern Arapahos, dwelling in what became Colorado and Kansas, had more interest in accommodating the new settlers. By the early 1860s, these settlers outnumbered the Southern Arapahos 10 to 1. The potential for conflict between the settlers and the Arapahos was great. The settlers' livestock was a temptation to the tribe, which often needed food, particularly after diseases brought by the settlers killed many hunters. When the Sioux and Cheyennes were goaded into skirmishes with U.S. government troops in 1854 and 1856, respectively, all Indians, including the Arapahos, were in danger of being fired upon by troops and civilians alike. The Arapahos were remarkably successful in avoiding the hostilities, however. They restricted their movements to areas away from trouble spots, and the men's lodges helped older leaders control the young warriors, who were eager to retaliate for the intruders' depredations.

Actually, the Arapahos were attracted to the settlements for practical reasons, and instigating hostilities would have been against their best interests. They came to trade for sugar and coffee, and the miners and settlers often gave them gifts and food. When Arapaho men went to war against the Utes, they left their families camped near the settlements for safety. Little Raven, the Southern Arapahos' intermediary chief in 1860, his interpreter Left Hand, and other distinguished warriors and leaders were invited to dinner parties by the business leaders and officials of the new towns.

The Arapaho leaders realized that they could not survive if the settlements continued to expand and threaten their hunting way of life. In 1860, Friday was heard to say plaintively, "The Great Spirit must have turned himself white and given white people power equal to his own." The intermediary chiefs asked for a new treaty, one that would guarantee them a place in their own country, where they would not be encroached upon by their white neighbors.

The Northern Arapahos, who reportedly numbered about 750 in 1861, wanted to stay north of the southern division. The Southern Arapahos, who numbered approximately 1,500, were now located primarily south of Denver. Both divisions had suffered severe population losses due to epidemics of smallpox and cholera and a shortage of food.

On February 18, 1861, Southern Arapaho Indian agent Albert Boone, a grandson of the famed frontier adventurer and settler Daniel Boone, held a council that was attended by some bands of Southern Arapahos and a few Cheyennes. He later reported that he had obtained their consent to the cession of most of their territory, reserving for them a small reservation on Colorado's Big Sandy Creek, away from areas of white settlement. The Cheyennes were to occupy the eastern half, and both divisions of the Arapahos the western. However, it is unclear whether the Arapahos understood the conditions of this treaty. Their chief interpreter, Left Hand, was not present. Moreover, the Sand Creek Reservation was not in a good location because the buffalo range was east and north of the reservation, and it seems unlikely they would have knowingly accepted this limitation. In any case, the northern division did not consent to the cession. By 1862, the Southern Arapahos were in such dire circumstances—due largely to the loss of buffalo at the hands of professional hunters—that, although there were no attacks on settlers,

Little Raven and other leaders could no longer keep their people from stealing the settlers' livestock.

Still, the Southern Arapahos worked to convince the Cheyennes to join them in remaining at peace with the whites. But, as hard as they tried, eventually they were unable to avoid conflict. In the spring of 1864, in retaliation for suspected rustling, Colorado troops destroyed a Cheyenne village, killing women and children, and, in another instance, shot two friendly chiefs. The Cheyennes replied in kind by attacking Colorado settlements. Officials there determined to forcibly drive all Indians away from areas of settlement and travel routes or, failing that, to exterminate them. The U.S. Army began to relentlessly attack Cheyenne villages, even those that had remained at peace.

These attacks brought retaliation from the Cheyennes and eventually involved the Arapahos. Initially, Little Raven, with Left Hand's help, tried desperately to avoid hostilities. They preferred to have the tribe depend increasingly on rations provided by the U.S. Army rather than risk hunting in settlement areas, where they were in danger of being attacked. Only small war parties of Arapahos made occasional raids.

John Evans, governor of the area (known as Colorado Territory), ordered all friendly Indians to designated areas near U.S. Army posts, where he guaranteed them safety, and ordered that Indians outside the designated areas be hunted down. Despite the governor's commands, U.S. Army officers frequently ordered Indians away from the posts. When Left Hand approached Fort Larned to offer to help retrieve lost army livestock, he was shot at, despite carrying a white flag.

In September, a large number of Arapahos, and some Cheyennes under Black Kettle, were ordered to camp near Fort Lyon on Big Sandy Creek, where they were guaranteed protection. All had pledged peace and delivered captives, arms, and booty. There were 500 Indians—about 110 tepees of Cheyennes, led by Black Kettle, and 8 tepees of Arapahos, led by Left Hand—already there. On November 29, 1864, Colonel John Chivington led a group of the Colorado militia in a surprise attack on the Indian encampment. Sixty-six Arapahos, mostly women and children, were killed. Left Hand was among them.

The main body of the Southern Arapahos, led by Little Raven, was camped several miles from Big Sandy Creek. This group—composed mostly of women, children, and the elderly—escaped south and took refuge in Kiowa and Comanche country. Most Arapaho men, upon hearing of the massacre, joined the Cheyennes in an all-out war against whites that lasted through the spring of 1865. Despite the Arapahos' peaceful disposition, the massacre, said Little Raven, "was too bad to stand."

In the summer of 1865, Arapaho leaders, with Little Raven as spokesman, began trying to arrange a truce and obtain a reservation where they could live undisturbed by whites. A council of federal officials, Southern Cheyennes, and Southern Arapahos came together on October 11, with Thomas Fitzpatrick's widow, Margaret, interpreting for the Arapahos at their request. The Southern Arapahos disassociated themselves from both their northern tribesmen and the Cheyennes, believing this would help them gain a reservation, and reiterated their desire for peace. Yet when the Cheyennes and the U.S. Army attacked each other during the winter of 1866–67, all Arapahos were at risk, for the army did not always distinguish between friendly and hostile Indians; moreover, most whites in the area considered the Arapahos as guilty as the Cheyennes for raids on settlements and wagon trains. Many Arapaho bands remained south of the Arkansas River, away from the fighting.

Observers at the Sand Creek Massacre had reported to newspapers in eastern cities that the militia had savagely mutilated men, women, and children, shot unarmed people in the process of surrendering, and committed other atrocities. In response to the public outcry, in order to avoid a costly and

In 1865, Little Raven, a Southern Arapaho chief, attempted to persuade the U.S. government to establish a reservation for his people. The federal government agreed to set up a reservation in Kansas, between the Arkansas and the Cimarron rivers, but the Arapahos did not like the area. They would eventually sign the Medicine Lodge Treaty in 1867, which provided for an Arapaho and Cheyenne reservation; it eventually was established in the western part of Indian Territory (present-day Oklahoma).

prolonged war with the Indians, President Andrew Johnson authorized a peace commission, despite the U.S. Army's objections. A treaty council was held at Medicine Lodge Creek in the fall of 1867.

Although some Cheyennes tried to discourage them, the Southern Arapahos attended the council and insisted on being dealt with separately from the Cheyennes. Little Raven and others wanted land in Colorado but eventually agreed to accept instead a reservation in Kansas, between the Arkansas and the Cimarron rivers, which they would receive when claims to the area were relinquished by other tribes. The Arapahos were dissatisfied with this area, however, and over the next two years they tried to persuade officials to grant them a reservation on the North Canadian River. They knew they would not be safe on the Arkansas River while the Cheyennes and U.S. troops continued to fight there and the U.S. Army persisted in attacking peaceful Indians. In the meantime, most of the Southern Arapahos fled to Oklahoma's Wichita Mountains to avoid contact with the U.S. Army.

In the winter of 1869, Little Raven came to Fort Sill (located in what is now Oklahoma) and, insisting that his people had always kept the peace, "surrendered" to the army, thus placing the Southern Arapahos under U.S. government protection. Officials at Fort Sill, convinced that the Arapahos' leaders could control the young warriors, sent Little Raven's group to the Camp Supply area, where it was still possible to hunt. President Ulysses S. Grant sent *Quaker* Indian agent Brinton Darlington to protect their interests and by executive order granted the Arapahos and Cheyennes a reservation together, in Oklahoma Territory on the Canadian River. Still hoping to disassociate themselves from the Cheyennes, the Southern Arapahos (who now numbered between 1,100 and 1,500) began to move to the vicinity of this new reservation and receive regular rations of sugar, coffee, and other goods.

By this time, most of the Northern Arapahos had withdrawn north of the Platte River, avoiding trouble and hunting the remaining buffalo in what is now Wyoming and Montana. They had also formed an alliance with the Sioux and Northern Cheyennes in an attempt to protect their hunting territory from incursions by whites and by other tribes.

Gold was discovered in Montana in 1862, and military posts and settlements inevitably followed. The result, aggravated by the Sand Creek Massacre, was a war that lasted from 1865 to 1868, at which time President Grant's peace commission met with the Northern Arapahos and their allies. Battered by their losses, the Northern Arapahos agreed to settle on a reservation with either the Sioux in the north or the Southern Arapahos in Oklahoma. The U.S. government agreed to close their military posts and to bar settlers and travelers from the tribes' hunting territory. The Northern Arapahos, however, were determined to obtain their own reservation in Wyoming, separate from that of the Sioux, and their leaders began to develop relations with U.S. Army officers at Fort Fetterman in order to achieve that goal.

The two most important Northern Arapaho leaders at the time were Medicine Man and Black Bear. They sent for Friday, an accomplished interpreter, to help them develop peaceful relations with the U.S. Army. After 1868, the Northern Arapahos began serving regularly as scouts for the U.S. Army and returned lost livestock to the troops. They also sought to establish peaceful relations with their longtime enemies, the Shoshones (who had accepted a reservation in Wyoming in 1868), and U.S. Army officers made appropriate arrangements to help them to that end. For a short time, the Northern Arapahos lived on the Shoshone Reservation, but there were clashes with trespassing settlers and miners along the Sweetwater and Popoagie rivers.

After Black Bear was ambushed and killed by a mob of settlers, Medicine Man led the tribe back to the vicinity of Fort Fetterman and resumed efforts to obtain a reservation solely for the Northern Arapahos. Game was so scarce that they depended on the U.S. Army's issues of canvas to make their tepees, cloth for their clothing, and rations for their sustenance. Medicine Man died in 1871 and was succeeded by Black Coal. In 1874, a combined force of U.S. troops and Shoshone warriors—the Arapahos' traditional enemies—made a surprise attack on a large Northern Arapaho camp. Most of their tepees, horses, and winter provisions were destroyed or stolen. Now the Northern Arapahos were totally dependent on the inadequate rations they obtained at Red Cloud, the Sioux Agency. Every ten days they received four days' rations. Many people died of illness and exposure in 1875 and 1876.

In the fall of 1876, the U.S. government called the Northern Arapahos, Northern Cheyennes, and Sioux together at the Sioux's Red Cloud Agency in Nebraska to negotiate the cession of the Black Hills in Wyoming and South Dakota. The tribes had little choice but to concede to the federal government's terms, although later leaders of the tribes argued that an insufficient number of signatures were obtained. Winter was coming; if they refused they would receive no provisions. Nonetheless, Black Coal told the officials from Washington, D.C., that the Northern Arapahos were unwilling to settle in Oklahoma, as the U.S. government had proposed. After he made a trip to inspect the Southern Arapahos' reservation on the Canadian River, Black Coal was more determined than ever to find a way for his people to remain in Wyoming.

Black Coal and other Arapaho leaders found a strategy that eventually proved successful: Virtually all their warriors signed on as army scouts in 1876 and 1877, assisting the U.S. Army in defeating Northern Cheyenne and Sioux bands that continued to refuse to settle on a reservation. Serving as "scout chiefs" enabled men to build reputations for generosity and bravery, to earn prestige and authority. The Northern Arapaho scouts wore U.S. Army uniforms, as well as feathered headdresses that testified to feats of courage and symbolized personal "war medicine" obtained in a vision quest. They received soldiers' pay, material provisions, rations, guns, and ammunition and could keep property seized from the enemy. This provided them with enough food and goods to enable them to be generous to others. The strategy devised by Black Coal and other Arapaho leaders proved effective: The scout chiefs gained the respect of

U.S. Army officers and obtained their promise to help the tribe settle in Wyoming. Sharp Nose rose to prominence as a leader of scouts, and he and Black Coal became the leading intermediary chiefs. To the Northern Arapahos, the scout uniform symbolized their bravery and generosity; to whites, it represented the Indians' trustworthiness and loyalty to the federal government.

In 1877, the Northern Arapahos were permitted to send a delegation to meet with President Rutherford B. Hayes in Washington, D.C. Black Coal, Sharp Nose, and Friday were selected to represent the tribe, and they were accompanied by U.S. Army officers. Black Coal told President Hayes:

> Last summer I went to see [the Southern Arapaho–Southern Cheyenne reservation] . . . Southern Arapahos, they told me it was sickly in that country. . . . They said a good many had died since they had been there. . . . When I came home I told my people what I heard; and they said . . . "Now you must push and talk for us, for we want to stay in this country [Wyoming]."[24]

With the U.S. Army's help, the three Northern Arapaho delegates obtained permission for their people to settle on the Shoshone Reservation in Wyoming. The delegates returned in triumph, wearing suits and medals given them by President Hayes, and riding in a black wagon filled with presents. To the Arapahos, the black paint symbolized a victory in an encounter with an enemy. In March 1878, Black Coal and Sharp Nose arrived on the Shoshone Reservation with their people.

4

Making Adjustments: The Northern Arapahos, 1878–1964

When the Northern Arapahos arrived at the Wind River Reservation in Wyoming in the spring of 1878, they faced new challenges. The first was how to survive when there was little game and the U.S. government provided only inadequate rations. The second was how to safeguard their new home when they had no treaty rights there and the legal owners, the Shoshones, did not want them as permanent residents. The last was how to survive as Arapahos, meeting their traditional obligations to kin and to supernatural forces, when the federal government's policy was to replace their culture with that of the mainstream non-Indian society.

These three problems were interrelated, for the U.S. government threatened to withhold food and remove the tribe from the reservation if they tried to maintain their Arapaho traditions. The Arapahos, however, felt that abandonment of their religious responsibilities would jeopardize both their survival and their

Black Coal, a Northern Arapaho chief, was instrumental in making it possible for his people to remain in Wyoming, instead of moving to the Southern Arapahos' reservation in Indian Territory. Black Coal and other Northern Arapaho leaders had some leverage in securing a reservation in Wyoming because many of his tribe's warriors served as scouts for the U.S. Army in conflicts with Northern Cheyennes and Sioux who refused to settle on reservations. In 1878, the U.S. government agreed to allow the Northern Arapahos to settle on the Shoshone Reservation.

political status on the reservation. To cope with any one of these problems, they had to cope with all three.

After defeating the Plains tribes militarily and confining them to reservations, the U.S. government had embarked on a program to "civilize" the Plains tribes by teaching them to farm,

Arapahos of every age wore moccasins, which were made of deer, elk, or buffalo skin. Shown here is a pair of boy's moccasins, circa late nineteenth century, from the Colorado Historical Society, Denver, Colorado.

The drum was a sacred symbol for the Arapahos and was painted red to symbolize old age and the elders' role as intermediaries between the people and the Creator. Shown here is a rawhide drum found at Bear Creek, Colorado.

Arapaho women made clothing like this child's buckskin dress by first soaking the animal hide. They would then scrape, soften, stretch, and finally tan the hide, before cutting the dress into the desired pattern and sewing it together with sinew pulled through holes punched with an awl.

Both Arapaho men and women wore leggings, which were originally made from the hides of buffalo, deer, or elk. However, when the Arapaho were forced to settle on reservations, they improvised by making some of their clothing from the canvas that was supplied to them by reservation agents.

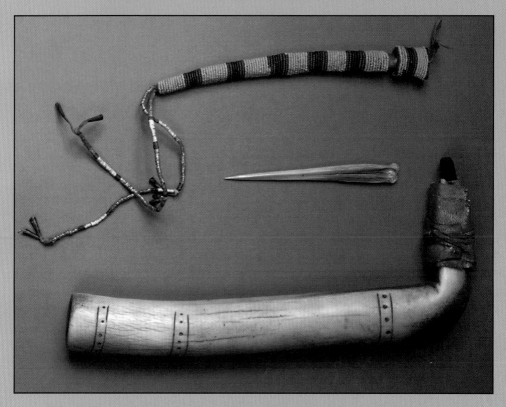

Plains Indians used scrapers, such as this one made from elk horn (bottom), to remove any excess meat or fat from the skin of an animal they planned to use to make clothing. Awls (middle) were also a part of the clothes-making process; they were used to punch holes in the hide so that different pieces could be sewed together to make clothing. Also shown here is an awl case.

Arapaho men sought supernatural power to guide them in certain situations by going on a vision quest. If the man was heading into war, he might protect himself by painting the vision he received during his vision quest on his shield. Shown here is a painted rawhide shield with feathers.

This eagle feather headdress belonged to Chief Yellow Calf, who was one of the Northern Arapahos' most prominent business council members during the early years of the Wind River Reservation. Headdresses often reflected feats of courage and symbolized personal "war medicine" that was obtained during vision quests.

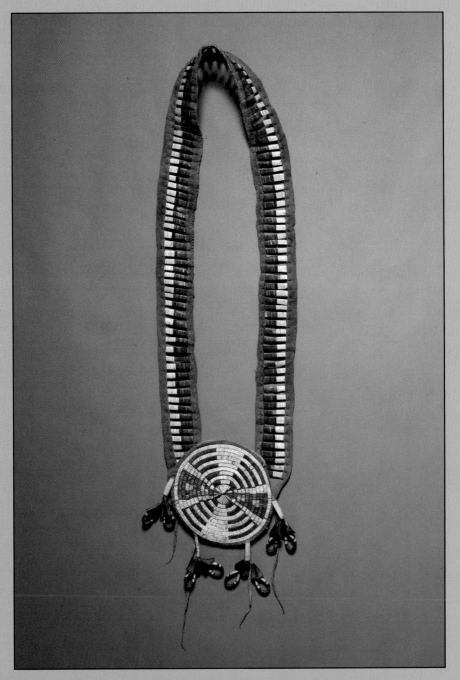

This late-nineteenth-century shoulder pouch, made from hide, deer hoofs, and porcupine quills, is part of the Newark (NJ) Museum's collection. Arapaho women often used these soft-skin pouches to hold small items such as quills and paints, and earrings, bracelets, and hair parters.

speak English, and accept Christianity. Yet Congress did not provide the funding for this endeavor. Instead, Congress passed legislation to reduce the Indians' land base, thereby making it more difficult for them to farm or otherwise develop their economy on the reservation. Agricultural instruction was minimal, schools inadequate, food rations insufficient, and most Indian agents, who were responsible for carrying out U.S. government policies on the reservations, were incompetent or corrupt. Arapaho leaders had to cope with all these problems.

Initially, most of the Northern Arapahos settled in two large camps of tepees, each camp ten miles apart: Black Coal's people on the southeast corner of the reservation, where the Wind and Popoagie rivers joined; and Sharp Nose's people on the Little Wind River, to the west of Black Coal's band. A third group, a smaller band led by Friday, also settled on the Little Wind, to the west of Sharp Nose's band.

The Arapahos' strategy for dealing with the problems of subsistence, recognition of their legal right to the reservation, and perpetuation of their cultural heritage was based on their belief in the cycle of the "four hills of life." On the reservation, as in earlier days, the roles of individuals changed as they aged. Along with each of the four hills of life, there existed particular challenges, as well as specific responsibilities and privileges. Responsibility for solving problems was undertaken by particular age groups, whose members worked together in customary ways. Elders were responsible for religious matters and supervised the middle-aged men who served as leaders in dealings with federal officials, teachers, and missionaries. Youths apprenticed themselves to the older men, taking on responsibilities gradually. Children were raised under the watchful eye of elders, whose prayers the parents still sought.

At the Wind River Reservation, most babies were born at home, and they were still named by elders to ensure that they would live a good, successful life. Parents continued to invite elders to eat with the family and pray for the child on various occasions. There were no longer cradles available for all babies, and new cradles were likely to be made of canvas, because deer hide was increasingly difficult to get. Hide clothing, too, was scarce and was worn only on ceremonial occasions. Women continued to make garments embroidered with beads, but they sold much of their work to museums and private collectors for money to buy food and supplies for their families.

As part of the federal government's "civilization" program, children were forced to attend either the boarding school that had been opened by the U.S. government or one run by the Catholic mission on the reservation. At the schools, the children's Indian clothing was taken from them, their long hair cut short, and they were punished for speaking the Arapaho language. Haircutting ceremonies came to replace the ear-piercing rituals of earlier times: A renowned warrior would cut the boy's hair, before a teacher had the chance to do so, and tell of his war exploits; in return he received gifts from the boy's parents.[25]

Games learned at school gradually replaced the older, traditional amusements, but children continued to ride ponies and listen to the stories told by their grandparents. At school, boys and girls were separated and taught different skills. Boys learned to care for livestock and do farm work, girls to sew and do housework. All learned English, the only language they were allowed to speak, and the "three Rs"—reading, 'riting, and 'rithmetic—that constituted the curriculum in most American schools of the period. Most Arapaho children started school when they were about nine years old and attended school for only three to six years. After leaving school, most began to work and got married. A few went to off-reservation boarding schools or stayed in school on the reservation to continue their education.

At boarding schools, youths were urged to reject Arapaho traditions and were often taught trades, such as tailor, bricklayer, or printer, which could not be practiced on the reservation. The Indian agents gave some young people special privileges and economic aid in an effort to enhance their status and undercut that of the elders, but the youths were ridiculed by their own people if they let an agent influence them.

Later, in 1917, the Episcopal Church would open a boarding school in the Arapaho community on the Little Wind River, where there were no harsh punishments and children were encouraged to express their Arapaho culture. Federal officials were appalled, but the new school was popular and drew students away from the other two schools on the reservation.

Parents still arranged some marriages for their young adult children, but gradually most young men and women came to choose their own spouses. The Indian agent or a clergyman performed the ceremony; those who participated in Indian ceremony marriages might be put in prison or have their food rations withheld. Although men were now forbidden to have more than one wife, the Arapahos still maintained their customary avoidance and joking relationships with their in-laws.

Young people in their twenties and early thirties were not considered fully mature, particularly because the young men could no longer earn prestige through warfare. Elders recognized that these were frustrating times for young people and tried to respond. They recruited youths into the religious lodges, relaxing the rules for admission and encouraging them to apprentice themselves to older individuals in the ceremonial hierarchy. They allowed young men to move up the age-based ranks much more rapidly than before, offering them a chance for prestige while still perpetuating the age hierarchy. In 1892, the average age of a Spearman had been thirty years; by 1910 it was only eighteen.

In the early twentieth century, the elders helped organize young people into social clubs according to their age and gender. The new organizations, such as a Christmas club and a summer entertainment society, resembled the traditional men's lodges in many ways. These clubs often helped the needy and sponsored community activities. Three singing groups, called drum groups because the singing was accompanied by a large kettledrum, were also organized, and the young men in them were apprenticed to older singers to learn traditional Arapaho songs. These groups sang at social club events.

The clubs, along with religious rituals, such as the Offerings Lodge and Pipe ceremonies, gave youths an alternative to the agents' plans and helped to reinforce the authority of the elders. Youths still depended on the elders' guidance and prayers for successful, satisfying lives. When they had difficulties, they often sought a new name from an elder. Old Man Sage told anthropologist Inez Hilger that in 1933 he gave his name to a young man "so that he could go straight."

Mature men in their forties and fifties struggled to make a living while still concentrating on meeting their ritual obligations. This age group included tribal leaders, who had the larger problem of finding ways to help their people.

It was not easy for these men to provide for their families. There were small farm gardens in the large camps, and the men herded livestock communally. Raising livestock was difficult, however, because the Indian agent could not prevent cattle rustling by people who were from off the reservation. Farming was not very productive, because the Arapahos did not have enough money to buy heavy equipment to harvest grain and the federal government was unwilling to assist them. Meanwhile, rations provided by the U.S. government became increasingly inadequate. In 1883, the Arapahos received four pounds of beef per person per week; by 1889, the ration had been reduced to one pound. After the turn of the twentieth century, the agent was instructed to give rations only to the old and disabled. Often the Arapahos' white neighbors and the agency personnel stole the rations before they could be issued. The resulting deprivation contributed to a high death rate: in 1885, there were 972 Northern Arapahos; in 1893, the population was down to 823. Arapaho men tried to earn money for their families by cutting and selling wood or hauling freight for the agency. Most had gone deeply into debt to the agency trader in order to get food.

To the mature men fell various official and political duties as well. When the Northern Arapahos first settled at Wind River, federal officials still expected to deal with chiefs. The traditional duties of the intermediary chief fell to Black Coal, Sharp Nose, and a few others who were known to officials by reputation. These leaders not only had outstanding war records but also were viewed as levelheaded and generous by their own people. Although these "council chiefs" did not have coercive powers, they were able to influence both their own people and the federal authorities. As participants in the system of age-ranked ceremonial lodges, they were subject to the authority of the elders but were also able to call upon the elderly ritual leaders to influence the tribe.

During the early years on the reservation, from about 1878 to 1904, these chiefs had the responsibility of finding solutions to the major problems facing the Arapahos: how to remain permanently at Wind River, how to get enough food to survive, and how to prevent loss of their culture. They set about to convince federal government officials that they were dependable allies who would remain at peace and cooperate with the "civilization" efforts. One of their more dramatic acts toward these ends occurred in 1881, when each Arapaho council chief sent one of his children to the Carlisle Indian School in Pennsylvania. Carlisle was a boarding school with a particularly rigorous program designed to bar all aspects of Indian culture and instead indoctrinate Indian children in the ways of Anglo-American society. The chiefs' children were, in effect, hostages guaranteeing the Arapahos' good conduct. Black Coal stated to federal officials that "[We] have given our children, whom we love. . . we wish also to assure you by this that we never more want to go on warpath, but always live in peace."

In their efforts to secure a place for Arapahos on the reservation, the men had to face consistent U.S. government efforts to decrease the size of reservation lands. They cooperated with the agent who, with the consent of Congress, was leasing reservation lands to non-Indian cattle raisers. They would accept individual ownership of land in 1900. More important, by agreeing to cede some reservation land in 1896 and 1904 they were able to get recognition of the tribe's legal right to the reservation.

The centerpiece of the U.S. government's policy to reduce reservation lands was the General Allotment Act, also known as the Dawes Act, passed by Congress in 1887. This law provided for reservation land to be divided into plots and given, or allotted, to each member of the tribe. Any land left over after all the people on a reservation had received their *allotment* plots was to be sold to non-Indians, and the income from that sale used for the benefit of the tribe as a whole. The intent was to make inexpensive land available to non-Indians, to end the communal, tribal ownership and use of reservation land, and to make it virtually necessary for Indians to become farmers on their own plots, as other Americans were.

In 1891 and 1894, Congress also passed legislation that allowed both allotted plots and unallotted tribally owned land to be leased to non-Indians. These measures were intended to provide income for Indian people, for Congress was determined to reduce spending on Indian affairs; the measures also served to satisfy the demands of cattlemen and settlers for more land. In addition, the legislation specified that a council of tribal leaders should approve the leases; this provision helped to strengthen the Arapaho chiefs. The agent began leasing land to cattle raisers in 1898.

In 1900, the chiefs agreed to Allotment, but only on the condition that stone markers be placed to establish Arapaho title to lands on which they had settled. Their allotments were between the forks of the Wind and Popoagie rivers and along the Little Wind River in the vicinity of that area's largest Arapaho camp.

At Wind River before Allotment, the Shoshones and Arapahos had been pressured to relinquish much of the 2 million acres of

Sharp Nose, who attained the rank of captain and is shown here in his army uniform, was a prominent scout for the U.S. Army during its campaign against the Cheyennes and Sioux. In 1877, Sharp Nose joined Black Coal on a trip to Washington, D.C., where they met with President Rutherford B. Hayes and lobbied for a reservation in Wyoming.

reservation land. In 1896, they ceded ten square miles in the northeast corner of the reservation. After Allotment, they were pressured to cede more. The Arapaho council chiefs maneuvered to keep as much land as possible in tribal ownership and to obtain official recognition of their right to live at Wind River. After the deaths of Black Coal in 1893 and Sharp Nose in 1901, the main Arapaho representative was Council Chief Lone Bear.

In the cession agreement, signed by the Arapahos as well as the Shoshones in 1904 (but not ratified until 1905), the tribes agreed to cede the lands north of the Big Wind River, about two-thirds of the reservation. The allotted lands were south of the river. In return for the cession, each Arapaho received a payment of $50. The U.S. government also agreed to establish a subagency at the eastern end of the reservation, which finally constituted the official recognition that secured the Arapahos' place at Wind River.

According to the 1904 agreement with the tribes, the federal government was to sell the ceded lands and use the proceeds to fund both a per-person payment and *irrigation* works so that the Shoshones and Arapahos could farm more effectively, purchase cattle, make school improvements; and be provided with supply rations. While payment was made, the U.S. government did not honor the rest of the terms of the agreement. The land was not suitable for farming, so homesteaders showed little interest in buying it. Cattle raisers preferred to lease land instead of buying it, so officials continued to lease the northern half of the reservation to whites.

To succeed in getting what they wanted, the council chiefs had to unify the Arapahos in support of their positions in order to present a solid front to the Shoshones, who did not want them to receive allotments, and to the federal authorities. The chiefs generated such support in the traditional way, by generosity. In prereservation days, a man who owned many horses would loan them to others for the hunt, and he would also distribute surplus meat from his own hunting efforts to needy families. On the reservation, the chiefs contributed to their followers' support by distributing food supplies given out by the agents.

Beef rations were delivered to the reservation "on the hoof." When the cattle arrived, the men ran them down and butchered them. The chiefs then distributed the meat. The chiefs received the hides of these slaughtered cows, which they sold, and also got other extra rations, such as up to one hundred pounds of flour per week. They used this extra income and food to support needy Arapahos and provide for visitors.

The council chiefs had other reserves to dispense as well. By 1886, Black Coal, Sharp Nose, and other lesser-known council chiefs had large hayfields and vegetable gardens along the rivers, where the Arapahos had constructed irrigation ditches as best they could. The chiefs' followers worked in the fields and shared the produce, and each chief used his own share to support the needy. Sharp Nose, employed as a scout at nearby Fort Washakie from 1881 to 1890, received scout's rations. He told his commander the amount would be sufficient if he were "selfish enough to use it himself," but instead he used it to "feed all his family and other people depending on him."

Black Coal had another strategy for providing food for his people. He welcomed the Catholic missionaries who came to the reservation in 1884 and helped them select land for gardens. Then he told the priests they would have to move and pay to use other lands; and each time they worked new land, he asked for a payment. In this way he obtained broken ground—soil ready for planting—for his followers to farm, as well as large stores of provisions. The Catholics did not object because they were competing with the Episcopal missionaries who had settled near Sharp Nose's group and were courting the Arapahos. Meanwhile, the council chiefs were successfully soliciting provisions from the Episcopal missionaries as well.

There was still another source of revenue over which the council chiefs exercised influence. The reservation lands north of Wind River were leased to non-Indian cattle raisers. The lease money was to be spent by the Indian agent for the benefit of the Indians. Every year, the council chiefs told the agent the tribe's consensus as to how the income should be spent—whether it should be used to buy seed, for example, or given to members of the tribe on an individual basis. Because the *Bureau of Indian Affairs* accepted these recommendations fairly consistently, the Arapahos respected the council chiefs and appreciated their importance. They provided for others and successfully influenced the federal government to provide support as well.

Black Coal and Sharp Nose were also adept at conveying to their fellow Arapahos the impression that federal officials regarded them highly. Council chiefs went to Washington, D.C., where they received medals and other gifts that symbolized the president's respect for them. Black Coal had been given a special outfit—a broadcloth suit with a watch and chain—by the secretary of the interior, and he made a point of wearing this on many public occasions. Sharp Nose, who had been General George Crook's head scout in 1876, wore his U.S. Army uniform; and he also named his son General Crook—a constant reminder to the Arapahos of his army connections.

The chiefs also worked to convince the agent and the missionaries that they were receptive to Christianity and that the Arapaho religion was not a threat to the U.S. government's "civilization" program. Chiefs personally welcomed, visited with, and attended the services conducted by missionaries. When the Arapahos had ceremonies, chiefs went to the U.S. Army commander at Fort Washakie, the military post on the reservation, and assured him the gathering was for peaceful purposes. Although the Arapahos had achieved legal recognition on the reservation in the agreement of 1905, in the years that followed the Arapahos' economic situation deteriorated and repressive measures against their culture continued. The U.S. government gradually decreased their rations. Those Arapahos who were employed by the federal government were usually paid with "purchase orders" that they could redeem only at a particular store, an arrangement that was often abused and resulted in the Indians being cheated. At the land cession council of 1904, U.S. government representatives had promised to build an irrigation system for the Arapahos and the Shoshones so that they could get higher yields from their allotment fields. Subsequently, the federal government reneged on this agreement and told the

Indians that they would have to pay to use water from irrigation ditches the U.S. government had built on the reservation. In 1907, Congress passed legislation to allow Indians to sell their allotments. Those without money to pay for irrigation of their farms were pressured by the agent to lease or sell their allotments to non-Indians.

Shortly after 1905, when an irrigation system was completed, most people moved from the three main camps and settled on their allotments in extended family clusters. When they first came to Wind River, they had lived in tepees. Later, unable to replace the worn-out skins used for tepee coverings, they began to live in canvas tents. In the summer, they built shelters covered with brush, called "shades," where they cooked, ate, and sometimes slept. On their allotment land, they kept gardens and small hay farms. In winter, almost everyone moved back to the three large camp communities that still remained—one in the forks of the Wind and Popoagie rivers, one on the lower Little Wind River, and the third on the upper Little Wind.

During the early part of the twentieth century, federal officials were no longer swayed by the Arapaho chiefs' reputations for bravery and declarations of peaceful intent. The Arapaho leaders had to change their strategy for dealing with U.S. government officials. From about 1906 to 1936, they presented themselves as "progressive" supporters of the federal government's policy to make Indians self-supporting. In the early twentieth century, the U.S. government encouraged them to elect a representative governing body, called a business council, in place of the chiefs' council. The chiefs agreed, at least outwardly. Now the lease book, which recorded who was leasing tribal land north of the Big Wind and how much income resulted, replaced the medal as a symbol of leadership.

Arapaho leaders made several trips to Washington, D.C., during this period as they tried to improve reservation conditions and gain more control over the reservation's natural resources, such as grazing land and mineral deposits. Money

In the early twentieth century, the Northern Arapahos agreed to a representative governing body, known as the business council, which traveled to Washington, D.C., several times during this period to improve reservation conditions and gain more control over the natural resources located on the reservation. Shown here, in 1908, (left to right) are Little Wolf, Lone Bear, Tom Crispin (standing), and Yellow Calf.

received from leasing land for cattle raising, oil production (which began in 1905), and some mining constituted the tribe's only source of income. Although the business council had the right to approve those who applied to lease their lands, federal officials now spent the lease income without regard for the tribe's wishes. Moreover, the lands were being leased for scandalously low prices. Members of the business council went to Washington, D.C., in 1908 and 1913, hoping to persuade federal officials to allow them to set higher prices for leases and to distribute the income to each person in the tribe.

In 1908, delegates from the business council persuaded the federal government to pay higher wages to Arapahos working on reservation ditches and roads. In 1913, they succeeded in getting the lease fees increased, and they convinced the U.S. government to use the lease income to buy the tribe its own cattle herd, as well as to build grist- and sawmills on the reservation. The cattle operation would provide a market for the hay grown by Arapaho farmers, and the mills would ensure fair prices for flour and lumber.

Business council members generally did not act on their own but consulted other Arapahos, particularly elders, before making council decisions. The elders reflected prevailing Arapaho opinion, but they also mobilized public sentiment behind specific goals of their leaders. The most prominent council members and spokesmen were Lone Bear (1854–1920), from the Wind–Popoagie River community, and Yellow Calf (1860–1938), from the Little Wind area. Both were exceptionally articulate in Arapaho and spoke enough English that they were not completely dependent on interpreters. Both had progressed through the men's lodges and served as council chiefs before the business council was formed. During the 1920s, younger men, who had apprenticed themselves to the older council members, began to become prominent.

Business council members, like the council chiefs before them, strove to demonstrate generosity to their fellow Arapahos. The Indian agent said of one that he "died in poverty" because of his charity. Until 1917, the council members received sizable quantities of rations and were paid to act as supervisors on agency work projects. With these supplies and funds, they aided the needy, sponsored tribal celebrations, and entertained visitors from other tribes. After 1917, they customarily received gifts of money from the people who leased tribal land, and these funds, too, they contributed to community activities.

Reciprocity held Arapaho social life together. Families helped one another with work, such as gathering hay and building, and shared food and other resources. Those who had paying jobs helped support those who did not. Some federal officials were dismayed that the more affluent and able-bodied Arapahos shared with the poor and weak. This, in their view, was not "progressive"; it was no way for individuals to "get ahead" and "make something of themselves." They were accustomed to people saving their individual earnings and using their accumulated money to advance their own standard of living. Council leader Lone Bear said of these officials: "They do not understand things, and they undertake to think for a man living here. They think their own way and think they can change the Indian in accordance with their own way of living. They think the Indians can make money and have [save] money like they can, but that is impossible." Sharing was the Arapaho way.

The role of elders in coping with reservation problems was no less important than that of middle-aged Arapahos. The elderly religious leaders aided the business council leaders in gaining support from the people, just as they had helped the council chiefs in the past. The ritual leaders often lectured the people in support of farming or other concerns of the leaders. In return, the council members worked diligently to mitigate the Indian agent's efforts to undermine the Arapaho religion. The 1908 delegation, for example, succeeded in convincing federal officials to cease their objections to the Offerings Lodge.

The ritual leaders also conducted ceremonies that helped to unify the people and motivate them to cooperate. The Keeper of the Sacred Pipe, for example, conducted Pipe ceremonies in which an individual vowed to make a prayer-sacrifice to the Pipe. Such vows were made known to the whole tribe, and the devotees were expected to be particularly kind and obliging to others. When there was conflict, ceremonial Grandfathers in the Offerings Lodge could defuse the situation simply by counseling or by pressing a pipe into the hands of a violent individual. The person would restrain himself rather than risk supernatural retaliation. Not long after the tribe settled at Wind River, one Arapaho man killed another. In order to preserve the tribe's reputation with federal officials for maintaining peace, the elderly ritual leaders persuaded the murderer to surrender to U.S. government authorities. They also dissuaded the victim's relatives from seeking revenge, as had been the custom.

The ritual leaders were generally quite flexible about permitting innovations in customs and ceremonies. In this way changes came about that eased people's adjustment to the new reservation conditions. For example, federal officials had issued orders to the agent to ban the Offerings Lodge ceremony altogether, because they objected to some of the forms of sacrifice practiced during the ceremony. To appease these officials, elders in 1890 eliminated the practice of self-torture. This concession made it possible for the lodge itself to continue. After the Arapahos settled on the reservation, the seven Water-Pouring Old Men did not select replacements. Instead, a larger group of knowledgeable elders supervised rituals. Although these ceremonial leaders also had personal *medicine power*, they did not pass it on to younger men or encourage them to obtain power in a vision quest. Perhaps they felt that such power was too dangerous to entrust to youths who were being educated by non-Indians.

New religions were introduced as well, not only Christianity but observances of Indian origin—the Ghost Dance and peyote ritual—that spread rapidly among Plains Indians in the late nineteenth and early twentieth centuries. Elders allowed the people to participate in new rituals as long as they continued to fulfill their obligations to the Sacred Pipe and kept it first in their hearts. The ritual leaders even worked to accommodate the new religious beliefs and practices while retaining their own religion. The Arapahos were friendly to Christian missionaries and accepted baptism, for example, without renouncing their own religious traditions.

The Ghost Dance ceremony, made popular by a Paiute Indian prophet in Nevada named Wovoka, promised the return of the buffalo and of believers' deceased relatives. The Arapahos heard about Wovoka and sent a delegation to learn how to practice the new religion. During the ceremony, people danced and prayed. Many had visions of a better life to come. The *Ghost Dance movement* flourished from 1889 to the early 1890s, after which it was gradually modified into another ceremony, the Crow Dance ritual. An individual would vow to sponsor the Crow Dance ceremony as part of a prayer. In this way, the new ceremony was more like the traditional lodge system. The Crow Dance was particularly popular among young people because it offered an opportunity for them to earn prestige.

In the peyote ceremony, people ingest the peyote cactus, which has hallucinogenic properties, as part of an all-night prayer service. The *peyote* appears to enhance the sensation of being in communication with the supernatural. Peyote had long been used by the Indians of Mexico and the American Southwest to enhance religious experiences. It was introduced to the Wind River Arapahos by youths who learned the ritual while visiting the Southern Arapahos in Oklahoma in the late 1890s.

The ritual authorities also found a way to use the business council to perpetuate their own influence and frustrate the Indian agents' efforts to undermine their authority. When it came time to elect the members of the council, the elders chose the men and then installed them in office with a specially cre- ated Drum ceremony. The singers brought the drum to the center of the camp. As they sang, the elders danced with great dignity around the drum with the men they had chosen. The drum was a sacred symbol. It was painted red, symbolizing old age and the elders' role as intermediaries between the people and the Creator. The sound of the drum, the eagle feathers attached to it, and other symbols used in the ceremony repre- sented the passage through the division between earth and sky, between the people and the Creator. The songs of the drum group were prayers for assistance in the difficult tasks ahead. The drum ceremony validated the leadership positions of the council members and helped generate support for them from the people. At the same time, the ceremony inspired council members to work on behalf of the people and to accept the guidance of the elders. The prayers of the elders were as necessary in reservation life as they had been in buffalo-hunting times. After the Drum ceremony, the new council members and their families held a feast and gave away property to the crowd. Then the results of the "election" were reported to the Indian agent.

In 1930, the federal government insisted that council members be elected by ballot. Even then, elders retained considerable influence over the selection process by expressing their support of certain candidates. The first people elected by ballot were those who had been chosen to serve on the council before 1930. Later, younger men, often World War II veterans, were elected. Following elections, elders installed the new council members with the Drum ceremony, and those elected accepted the authority of the elders just as those appointed earlier had. Elected council members were also expected to pursue the goals of their constituents, as the appointed leaders had in the past.

The elders remained flexible about innovations. They created, for example, new positions of responsibility for rituals, which gave ceremonial authority to more people. They also divided the responsibilities of people in different authority positions as a way of limiting the growing powers of the council. The business council, for example, managed relations with non-Indians. The elderly ritual leaders did not serve on the council; they directed religious life. Thus the elders were not vulnerable to criticism from people who were annoyed with a decision made by the council. A dance committee supervised club activities; the committee was composed of elders and their younger apprentices, who were chosen by the elders before 1951 but were elected thereafter.

The elders also were intimately involved in the Arapahos'

(*continued on page 74*)

The Arapahoe Ranch

In 1937, the Shoshone tribe won a $4.5 million judgment against the United States because the federal government violated the 1868 Fort Laramie Treaty by allowing the Arapahos to settle on the Shoshone Reservation. Congress set aside $1 million of the judgment fund to buy land for the tribe. The U.S. government also pressured the Arapaho tribe to borrow $500,000 from the Shoshone fund to purchase a large ranch and several smaller ranches that bordered the northeast corner of the reservation, twenty miles northwest of Thermopolis, Wyoming. The Shoshones paid an equal amount for joint ownership of the land, but the Arapaho tribe became the sole owner of the cattle ranch subsequently established there. The Arapaho tribe has paid grazing fees to both tribes' accounts since the ranch began operating. The Arapahos acquired federal rehabilitation funds to buy livestock and equipment, and the ranch began operating in 1941 with 4,939 head of cattle. By 1947, the Arapahos had paid back their loan from the Shoshones with 4 percent interest.

Arapahos had experience in ranching. In 1931, they already had two cattle associations for the cooperative management of individual herds. Indian riders were hired to oversee the stock that grazed collectively on distant parts of the reservation. By 1939, there were thirty-one Arapahos who had small cattle herds of between twenty and thirty head. At the time of the ranch purchase, however, the Bureau of Indian Affairs insisted on a non-Indian manager and non-Indian ranch hands, because U.S. government officials believed that non-Indians were more likely to operate a profitable business. The Arapaho Business Council struggled against this attitude and was offended that they owned the ranch but had never been invited to see the manager's house. "We are humans, too," remarked one business council member.

In 1948, they obtained the authority to select the manager and make policy decisions. The business council instructed the manager to sell livestock by public auction rather than private negotiation, which had been the practice. In 1951, they began to hire managers who had worked successfully with Indians, and they gave preference to Arapaho cowboys when they hired ranch hands. By the 1950s, the herd had doubled and was profitable enough to pay an annual dividend to each Arapaho. In 1964, the council selected three tribal members as a board of trustees to oversee the ranch.

The ranch, with about 363,000 acres of grazing land and 4,500 acres of irrigated land, has operated at a profit most years. The ranch is stocked with Herefords: two-year old heifers, yearling heifers, yearling steers, and bulls. The horses used on the ranch are raised and trained there and some are sold to the general public.

The ranch employs up to 120 workers, most seasonally. The majority of the ranch hands are Arapahos, but there are a few Shoshones, Indians from outside Wyoming, and non-Indians. There are several different kinds of jobs: line rider, horse breaker, horse wrangler, cow foreman, irrigator, hay equipment operator, mechanic, cook, bookkeeper, and cowboy. In the winter, workers feed the cattle, doctor the stock, fix fences, and rack hay. In the summer, they brand cattle and cut hay.

The Arapaho tribe has preferred to support this communally owned cattle ranch rather than establish individuals in the ranching business. As one Arapaho leader put it, "If everyone is allowed to expand to the extent that they will be economically [well] situated, only a few will survive. The rest will have to go somewhere else." On the other hand, Shoshone tribal members have preferred to establish small individually owned ranches. In fact, the number of individually owned Arapaho cattle ranches has dropped since the establishment of the ranch. The ranch has employment policies that permit workers to take time off to participate in ceremonies without endangering their jobs. In the early years of ranch ownership, many Arapahos did not view the ranch as theirs. They believed the federal government owned it. In fact, federal officials presented the ranch as a kind of gift from the U.S. government rather than an investment of tribal funds. Gradually, Arapahos identified with the ranch and formulated tribal goals for it. The Arapahoe Ranch is a source of pride for Arapahos today, even though in recent years it has not always paid a dividend due to high costs and low prices for cattle.*

* Adapted from Loretta Fowler, "The Arapahoe Ranch: An Experiment in Cultural Change and Economic Development," *Economic Development and Cultural Change* 21, 3 (1973): 446–64.

(*continued from page 71*)

continuing struggle to obtain control of reservation resources. Their involvement was made possible by new federal policies toward Indians initiated in 1934, during the first term of President Franklin Roosevelt. With John Collier as commissioner of Indian affairs, the programs known as the *Indian New Deal* constituted a complete reorganization of the relationship between Indians and the federal government. Many tribes now were able to form their own governing bodies that would increase their jurisdiction over reservation affairs. The federal government also took steps to protect land already owned by tribes and to hear Indian claims concerning rights to natural resources, including land and water, and for payment still due on previous land cessions. There was at last a favorable climate for remedying the wrongs done to Indians in past years.

The Shoshone and Arapaho people on the Wind River Reservation refused to organize a constitutional government but moved quickly to take advantage of the new policies. In 1927, Congress had passed legislation to allow the Shoshones to file a suit in the court of claims for damages against the United States for locating the Arapahos on the Shoshone Reservation in violation of the Shoshones' treaty. When the Shoshones won their suit in 1937, the Arapahos benefited also. The reservation's name was changed from Shoshone to Wind River, and a portion of the monetary award was used to buy more land for both tribes. The Shoshones were awarded more than $4 million, $1 million of which Congress decreed would be used to purchase land. In 1940, at the discretion of Congress, the portions of the reservation that had been ceded in 1905 but not sold were restored to the tribes by the secretary of the interior, and much of the land owned by non-Indians was purchased from them by the tribes. In a plan worked out in Congress, the Arapahos borrowed $500,000 from the Shoshones, who used the remainder of their land-purchase fund, and both tribes bought these lands. Thus, reservation resources were greatly expanded.

The business councils of both tribes then began a campaign to bring about increased production from oil wells on these lands. Federal authorities had not adequately supervised the companies that leased oil-rich Wind River land. Because the companies were not required to do test drillings, because they sometimes capped wells instead of continuing to produce from them, and because officials had not prevented sales and sub-leases to speculators, the tribes had lost a considerable amount of potential income over the years. The Arapaho and Shoshone councils sent delegations to Washington, D.C., to convince the secretary of the interior to authorize increased production. In 1939, the Wind River delegates accomplished their goal.

Next, the two business councils fought the Department of the Interior for the right to obtain per-person payments of the income due to both tribes. Up to this time, at Congress' direction, the income from royalties from oil and leases on tribal land had gone into the U.S. Treasury, where it was administered by the secretary of the interior on behalf of the Shoshones and Arapahos. The secretary had directed that the money be spent to improve agency buildings, pay salaries of non-Indian agency employees, and for other purposes of which the tribes did not necessarily approve. He had opposed giving the money directly to Indian families, saying they would not spend it wisely. The business councils wanted the money to go to the people because there was great poverty at Wind River. All Arapaho households needed money to pay for food, health care, and other needs. In 1936, the Arapaho population was 1,128, more than twice what it had been at the turn of the century. This rapid growth was stretching meager resources to the limit. Housing was inadequate: A 1940 survey of 218 Arapaho households by the Bureau of Indian Affairs showed about a third still living in tents, another third in single-room log houses, and a final third in log or frame houses with two rooms or more. There were serious health problems such as tuberculosis. All but ten Arapaho families were receiving some form of financial support from U.S. government relief programs.

In 1947, a delegation from the Arapaho and Shoshone business councils appeared before Congress. To influence legislators, they referred to the number of men from Wind River who had been in military service during World War II and to the many injustices the tribes had suffered under federal

Work Relief Projects on the Wind River Reservation

During the Great Depression, from 1933 to 1942, Arapahos and Shoshones worked on work relief projects on the Wind River Reservation. The federal government financed the work and the federal official appointed as superintendent of the reservation managed the projects. Arapaho men were hired, often for $1 a day, to build roads, fight fires, do forestry work, and construct buildings for the Civilian Conservation Corps-Indian Division (C.C.C.). Work relief generally consisted of labor-intensive, low-overhead projects. Arapahos also obtained income by using their teams of horses on these projects. Project managers generally were non-Indians but some Arapahos served as camp managers. The Arapaho Business Council pressed the federal government to hire mostly Indians from Wind River, rather than elsewhere, in order to obtain the most employment possible for Arapahos and Shoshones.

Workers lived in camps located in the areas where the work occurred. Single men lived together in camps, where they participated in such activities as boxing, basketball, baseball, and card playing. Married workers lived with their families in other camps, where women cooked and otherwise maintained the household. In the evening, the people played games, such as the hand game (or button game), and told traditional stories. In the hand game, two teams sat facing each other. One team had a "button" (made of stone or wood, usually) that the players tried to keep hidden from the other team. Hand game songs were sung while the players kept time with the drum by hand and arm movements. The other team had to try to guess where the button was, as their opponents moved it from one hand to the supervision. The delegation succeeded in convincing Congress to allow two-thirds of the tribal income to be distributed in regular per-person payments. In 1956, the proportion allocated for individual payments was increased to 85 percent of tribal income. The remaining fifteen percent was to be administered by the business council and spent primarily on helping the needy, for legal fees incurred in defending

other or from person to person. If one side guessed correctly, they got tally sticks and took a turn trying to hide the button. If they guessed incorrectly, they gave up tally sticks. Property was waged on the outcome.

The Works Progress Administration (WPA) also sponsored the development of community gardens and work projects for women, which included mattress making and handiwork (hide-tanning and quilt making) for older women. Younger women learned from the older ones so that the projects helped perpetuate tribal artistic traditions. The Arapaho tribal government, with assistance from the C.C.C. and the Works Progress Administration, operated a vegetable-canning plant that hired young women to process the produce of local farmers. It was hard work. As one woman explained, "We had to go out in the field . . . and pick all the vegetables and . . . load them up and bring them back and clean them" then work the canning machinery.

All these projects helped provide Arapahos with income during the difficult depression years, when their lease income fell and unemployment was high throughout the state and the nation. During these times, work relief projects provided assistance to Americans throughout the country.*

* Adapted from Brian Hosmer, "'Dollar a Day and Glad to Have It' Work Relief on the Wind River Indian Reservation as Memory," in *Native Pathways: American Indian Culture and Economic Development in the Twentieth Century* (Boulder, Colo.: University Press of Colorado, 2004), 283–307.

tribal interests, and to pay the operating expenses of the tribal government.

After the Arapahos began to receive individual payments, their living standards improved tremendously. Between 1947 and 1951, 87 new homes were built, most households installed electricity, and most families no longer had to rely on relief monies.

In 1946, Congress established the *Indian Claims Commission* (ICC) to rule on charges brought by Indian groups who argued that they had not received adequate payment when their land was sold or that their property, including mineral and other resources, had been mismanaged. In 1955, the combined Northern and Southern Arapaho divisions, together with the Cheyennes, filed a claim with the ICC for violation of the 1851 Treaty of Horse Creek and for inadequate compensation for land subsequently taken from them. They won the case in 1961 and were awarded a multimillion-dollar judgment. The Northern Arapaho business council and the tribal elders, who had worked jointly on the case, gained considerable prestige; the authority of both was validated by the lawsuit's success. In the twentieth century, the Northern Arapahos not only maintained continuity with their past in a very important way but also accomplished practical goals that improved their lives.[26]

5

Assimilation Tested: The Southern Arapahos, 1871–1964

The Southern Arapahos numbered about 1,650 when they all finally settled with the Cheyennes at Darlington Agency on the North Canadian River in 1870. In many ways, their experience in Indian Territory (Oklahoma) resembled that of their northern kin; in important ways it was different. The Southern Arapahos, for example, had an adequate food supply for a number of years. Some buffalo still roamed the reservation and its vicinity, and the tribe separated into several bands to hunt them in late fall and again in summer. After these hunts they returned to the agency, where Indian agent Brinton Darlington had planted corn, melons, and garden vegetables that the Arapahos assumed were theirs to take. The agency was staffed by members of the Society of Friends, or Quakers, who sought to teach the Indians farming and cattle raising through example rather than by force. The Arapaho chiefs tried to oblige Darlington, whom they liked, and they quickly

(continued on page 82)

79

Reflections from Arapaho Artist Carl Sweezy

Arapaho artist Carl Sweezy and writer Althea Bass collaborated on a book, *The Arapaho Way: A Memoir of an Indian Boyhood*, about Sweezy's childhood recollections of his experiences growing up on the reservation. Sweezy was born in 1881 and named "Black." He had three older brothers. His father was one of the Indian Police and his mother died when he was small. After her death, he was placed in a boarding school on the reservation, first in the Mennonite Mission School at Darlington and then later he joined one of his brothers in school at Halstead, Kansas, where the Mennonites had a farm and a school for Indian children. At Halstead, his brother had taken the name of Fieldy Sweezy, the station agent there. The U.S. government policy was for children to adopt English names and to use their father's surname, so he took the name of Carl Sweezy. He returned from Halstead when he was fourteen.

At the time, noted anthropologist James Mooney was conducting research on the reservation and he hired Carl to draw and do restorative painting on artifacts Mooney purchased for the Smithsonian Institution. Carl also worked as an illustrator for anthropologist George Dorsey and found his calling as an artist—he eventually supported himself by selling his paintings of Indian life. Many of his paintings are part of prominent collections, including that of the Heard Museum in Phoenix, Arizona.

Carl Sweezy painted Arapaho life as he saw it during his boyhood or as it was described to him by elderly Arapahos. He painted scenes of daily life: the interior of a tepee, boys playing games, and women tanning hides. His work includes scenes of dances, the Sun Dance ceremony, and peyote ceremonies. Relying on stories he heard as a child, he painted scenes of buffalo hunting and battles against enemies from other tribes, non-Indian buffalo hunters, and U.S. troops.

In his book with Bass, Carl described his family's tepee and furnishings. The tepee door faced east and by the entrance were boxes from the trader's store containing sugar, salt, flour, and coffee. Around the circumference of the tepee were the beds, which were low wooden frames with mattresses of willow twigs held together by thongs. One end was long enough to make a backrest supported by a tripod. On the south were the women's beds. On the west side was his father's place and here he kept his shield, arrow quiver, medicine bundle, saddle, and hide or cloth painting of his war exploits. The boys and any visitors had beds on the north side. In the center was the fire, a pit lined with stones with kindling on top. A pot of meat and vegetables was kept warm there all day. Each family member had a plate made of tin, wood, or china, and a spoon and cup. His mother kept robes and moccasins in parfleches; pots and kettles in boxes; and clothing, toys, and tools under the beds so that the tepee would be neat and orderly. Bags of dried food hung from the tepee poles. There was a smaller fire in the tepee where cedar or sage was burned as a smudge to purify in a religious sense his father's arrows and mother's robes. In the winter, his family's tepee was on low ground near the river where it was sheltered from cold winds. In the summer, they moved to higher ground to benefit from cool winds. They might also move to find better pasture, wood, or water. His father hunted large and small game (deer, bear, raccoon, wolf, and badger); he could sell the skins to the traders. On the days that the agent distributed beef and other food, or when the goods promised in the Medicine Lodge Treaty were distributed, the family would dress in their best clothes and ride to the agency.

At school, Carl worked at farming, dairying, construction, and cutting hay. By learning English, he and other students were able to obtain employment at the agency. Jobs included interpreting, clerking, working in the sawmill, cutting hay and wood, and building fences. Keeping to a schedule was difficult for students and workers. At the agency a bell was rung at 7 A.M., noon, and 6 P.M. to remind Arapahos and Cheyennes to go to work, eat, and stop work.

Carl also expressed to Bass his feeling that Arapahos were misunderstood and treated unfairly by non-Indians. They were described as "savage" because they made war and practiced polygyny; yet he read that the people in the Bible did the same. Arapaho men were accused of being lazy; yet hunting was difficult work. The federal government tried to force them to cut their hair and abandon their customs; yet the Medicine Lodge Treaty did not prescribe these changes. The United States broke the treaty; yet Arapahos kept their promises.*

---

* Information adapted from Althea Bass, *The Arapaho Way: A Memoir of an Indian Boyhood* (New York: Clarkson N. Potter, Inc., 1966).

(*continued from page 79*)
learned to plant and supervise work on small patches of corn
and melons.

As with the Northern Arapahos, however, many cultural
traditions endured in the first two decades of reservation life.
Women continued to give birth at home, and the parents sponsored feasts to name their infants and to announce their first
successful attempt to walk. Boys practiced hunting with small
bows and arrows, and girls played with toy tepees and learned
to dress and decorate hides. A boarding school was established
at the agency, but parents were reluctant to let their children
live there, especially since the school quickly became known for
having a high death rate due to malaria and to other illnesses
that stemmed from an inadequate sewage-disposal system. For
some time the agent was able to recruit only orphans to attend
classes. Mennonite missionaries (a Swiss-Dutch Protestant
sect) also established a school at Darlington, and another at
Cantonment (now called Canton), fifty miles northwest at the
site of a former U.S. Army garrison, but these schools also
failed to attract students. Parents resented the schools' practices
of cutting the children's hair and forcing them to give up their
good buckskin clothing for school uniforms. The children were
not used to following schedules, so that a teacher had to walk
through the camps blowing a cow horn to summon them to
class.

In 1879, Southern Arapaho chief Little Raven, his successor
Left Hand (no relation to the Left Hand killed at Sand Creek),
and other chiefs who were heads of the Arapaho bands decided
to send their children to the Carlisle Indian School in
Pennsylvania as proof of their loyalty to the United States.
Following their example, other parents gradually began to send
their children to one of the three reservation schools. There, the
boys learned how to raise crops and herd cattle, and the girls to
sew and make clothing from cloth distributed to families every
year. (In the Medicine Lodge Treaty of 1867, the federal government had guaranteed to distribute clothing, household

utensils, and other goods to the Arapahos and Cheyennes for twenty-five years, or until 1892.) Children were paid for their work at the agency school. Their parents could take them out of school to participate in ceremonies, such as the Offerings Lodge. The Mennonites sent approximately twenty Arapaho children every year to Halstead, Kansas, where they all lived on a farm with a Mennonite family, learning English (and some German, since most Mennonites were of German origin) and farming methods. By 1890, most Arapaho children had at least a rudimentary knowledge of English.

Marriages were still arranged or, if they resulted from a courtship, approved by the bride's and groom's families with an exchange of gifts, which usually included horses. As at Wind River, the men seldom had more than one wife, primarily because one wife could now manage the household tasks; there were, for example, fewer hides to be tanned than in buffalo-hunting days. Pressure from the Indian agent also influenced Arapaho men to give up *polygyny*.

With the buffalo nearly extinct by this time, men hunted deer, quail, turkey, and prairie chicken to supplement the weekly beef ration, which was enough to last only about four days. A family that could not afford food or find game would have little but water for the remaining three days. So men worked at what jobs they could find to earn cash and did their best to grow corn in a region where recurrent droughts and other factors made farming unreliable. A few cared for small herds of cattle, and most sold wood and hauled freight for the agency. Some men were hired at the agency as herders, black-smiths, or police. A few women also worked at the government school in domestic jobs. The yearly distribution of cloth and clothing helped substitute for the scarcity of hides. The men wore cloth shirts with their breechcloths, leggings, and moc-casins. The men were still more comfortable in their tradi-tional clothing, and those who received trousers would often cut out the seat and use them as leggings. Men still spent much

Reservation agents handed out ration tickets to Arapaho women that determined the amount of flour and other food items a family would receive on a given day. Ration tickets were often carried in a pouch, like the one shown here.

time repairing ceremonial equipment and making bows and arrows.

Women now made their tepee covers out of the yearly issue of canvas and made dresses and leggings from cloth as well. Some families began living in tent-houses instead of tepees. These were built by stretching canvas over a wooden house frame. Missionary women taught many Arapahos how to use a sewing machine. Women carried the family's ration tickets in a pouch made just for that purpose. The tickets determined the amount of flour and other food the family received on issue day. It was the responsibility of the women to cut the beef into strips and dry it in the sun and wind so that it did not spoil.

Women also continued to gather wood and wild plants. They cooked cattail roots in stews and dried wild grapes, cherries, and roses. The women tanned cowhide and sold the hides to traders to get cash. Gradually, they began to purchase bedsteads, tables, and stoves for their tepees or tent-houses.

The Southern Arapahos' middle-aged leaders still played an important role in the 1870s. Band headmen took responsibility for overseeing the weekly distribution of beef to their people. The agency staff let a steer out of the corral and each headman directed the men of his band in running the animal down, butchering it, and then distributing the meat. Headmen and chiefs got extra rations and goods, which they used to support needy band members. Before the railroad reached Darlington, the agency hired the bands to transport, by wagon train, the supplies needed at the agency. The band headman was the leader of his band's freight train; and the freighting jobs were rotated among the bands. The men's lodge societies continued to exist, functioning to maintain order in the camps.

The Arapaho leaders' goal during this early reservation period was to convince the U.S. government to separate them from the Cheyennes, which they hoped to achieve by cooperating with U.S. government officials and programs. In contrast to the Cheyennes, who had sporadic violent confrontations with non-Indians and who went to war again in 1873–74, the Arapahos protected the agency and escorted U.S. Army troops through dangerous country. They became accustomed to demanding "gifts" from the whites in return for their services— and they usually got what they asked. John Seger, an agency employee, remarked: "We had learned to trust the Arapahos and yet some of them, as they saw how much we depended upon them, became very exacting and expected a great many privileges. They took the liberty of entering employees' houses whenever they chose to do so, and were often annoying. They felt we owed them a great deal—and we did."[27]

The Arapahos went out of their way to cooperate with the

U.S. government's agricultural program. They would break the soil with butcher knives when promised farm equipment did not arrive in time. They struggled to build up herds due to constant thefts of Indian livestock by non-Indian desperadoes in what was still the unsettled frontier of the United States.

Because U.S. government officials considered houses more "civilized" than tepees, they pressed some Arapahos to move into them, even though the tepees were often better insulated and more comfortable. Important chiefs agreed to accept houses, and some even paid to have them constructed. Little Raven accepted the abandoned hospital building at Cantonment and, although he continued to spend most of his time in his tepee, he planted forty acres of corn there. After a house was built for the chief Big Mouth, he pointed out that the house had only four rooms and he had seven wives, each of whom demanded a room for herself. He decided to move his camp close to the house and to store his hides and keep his dogs in it.[28]

The Southern Arapaho leaders' efforts resulted in an agreement in 1873 between a delegation of their chiefs and the secretary of the interior to establish separate reservations for the Southern Cheyennes and Southern Arapahos, but Congress never approved the agreement. Arapaho leaders kept trying until their reservation was abolished in 1892.

The elders continued to fulfill their traditional responsibilities; they conducted the lodge ceremonies and the Sun Dance and they continued to instruct and encourage their juniors. Elderly men who had supernatural power to cure tried to heal their people, who had been made sick from water polluted by wastes from a nearby U.S. Army post and by malaria transmitted by swarms of mosquitoes that infested the area.

Meanwhile, rationing was slowly phased out, as it had been at Wind River. By 1883, Brinton Darlington's successor as agent, John Miles, began to lease reservation grazing land to non-Indian cattle raisers and distribute the resulting "grass money" income to the Arapahos and Cheyennes twice a year. In

1885, however, Cheyenne opposition moved President Grover Cleveland to expel the cattle raisers. Shortly afterward, the surrounding non-Indian population began to put pressure on the federal government to open the reservation to settlement by non-Indians.

In 1889, the Southern Arapahos learned of a prophet far to the west who had learned in a vision how the Indians could bring back the lost buffalo herds and their former way of life. The Arapahos were desperate. Their numbers had been reduced, primarily by deaths from malaria, to 1,137. The United States had kept none of the promises made in the Medicine Lodge Treaty of 1867.

Hearing that the Northern Arapahos were already practicing the Ghost Dance, Black Coyote went to Wind River to learn about the ritual. Smithsonian Institution ethnologist James Mooney, who studied the Ghost Dance extensively, described Black Coyote as "a man of contemplative disposition, much given to speculation on the unseen world." Black Coyote was intensely religious. When he was a young man, several of his children had died. As he prayed for the health of his remaining children, he had a vision in which he was instructed to cut seventy pieces of skin from his upper body as a sacrifice to accompany his prayers. He completed the sacrifice, and the rest of his children survived.[29]

Black Coyote returned to his people from Wyoming in the spring of 1890 and began to lead Ghost Dance ceremonies. In the fall, Sitting Bull, a Southern Arapaho who had been living with the Northern division, arrived at Darlington and began to lead the devotees. Sitting Bull was able to hypnotize people into a trance by the use of a feather. In their trance state they saw their deceased relatives in another, better world where Arapahos hunted buffalo again and prospered in their traditional ways. People danced with feathers of the crow, eagle, or magpie. They wore painted designs representing these birds or the mythological Thunderbird, which caused thunder and lightning, or of other celestial objects that appeared to them in trances. The wings of the birds, messengers from the supernatural world above, would help symbolically to carry the devotee upward to facilitate a trance.

Parents, desperate to see their deceased children, joined the new religion by the hundreds. The Ghost Dance also encouraged the revival of handcrafts and the perpetuation of the Sun Dance and prayer with the Sacred Pipe. Southern Arapahos continued to make pilgrimages north to Wyoming to pray with the Pipe. Through faithful performance of the Ghost Dance, devotees could hasten the replacement of the world they now knew with the one they saw in their visions.

While the Arapahos had been learning the Ghost Dance, events were taking place that would make their situation even more grave. Indian lands were coveted by would-be settlers. As a result, in 1887, Congress passed the General Allotment Act, which affected all reservations. Officials began to plan the division of the reservations into small sections that would be given, or allotted, to individuals. Land that remained unallotted was to be sold to non-Indians. In October 1890, a commission came to negotiate with the Cheyennes and the Arapahos for the allotment of the reservation and the sale of "surplus" land. The Indians were shocked and dismayed. They had been promised possession of their lands for as long as they wanted them. They knew that their only hope of becoming fully self-sufficient was to raise cattle and that they needed all of the reservation land to support a cattle business. Now they were being forced to accept the breakup of the reservation and the loss of land on which their very survival depended. The federal government commission presented them with a document in which they had to agree to the cession of much of the reservation. Officials threatened them with the complete cutoff of rations, bribed their interpreters, promised them they would be supported in grand style, and forged many signatures on the cession agreement. Despite evidence of fraud, Congress approved the cession on March 3, 1891.

Shown here is an Arapaho Ghost Dance, circa 1893. The Ghost Dance ceremony, which spread throughout the West thanks largely to a Paiute prophet named Wovoka, quickly became a part of Arapaho religious life. The most prominent Southern Arapaho devotees were Black Coyote and Sitting Bull, who began to lead Ghost Dance ceremonies on the tribe's reservation in 1890.

Principal spokesman Left Hand (who succeeded Little Raven, who died in 1890) and other chiefs had meanwhile become converts to the Ghost Dance religion. Now, faced with the threat of cession, Left Hand asked Sitting Bull for advice. Sitting Bull believed the message of Wovoka—that a new world was coming very soon. The troublesome white people would be barred from this world, and all would be as it was before they came. He told Left Hand to sign the agreement but to obtain the best terms for the tribe that he could. Despite bitter opposition from many Cheyennes, Left Hand and the other Arapaho leaders agreed to the cession. They did, however, struggle to obtain larger allotments and more money as compensation to the tribes.

As he signed, Left Hand said, "I see the new land coming." Even after the prophecy failed to materialize, many Arapahos continued to dance for several years, for they believed the Ghost Dance ritual would prevent sickness and would lead to a better life sometime in the future. By the 1920s, however, the Ghost Dance served primarily a social rather than religious purpose.

After the cession of 1891, the lands of the Cheyennes and the Arapahos were opened for settlement by non-Indians. The original reservation had been about 4 million acres. Each Cheyenne and Arapaho was allotted 160 acres. These allotments, totaling a little more than 500,000 acres, were then put into *trust* status. This meant that they were controlled by federal officials on behalf of the Indians and for twenty-five years they could not be sold or taxed by Oklahoma Territory. The remaining 3.5 million acres were opened for settlement by non-Indians. In compensation, the federal government agreed to pay the tribes $1.5 million, or about 40 cents an acre. Of this amount, the tribes were to receive $500,000 paid in equal amounts to each person; in actuality they received less. The remaining $1 million was placed in the U.S. Treasury to earn 5 percent annual interest. The tribes were to receive the interest each year in payments that amounted to less than $20 per person.

The land allotted to the Southern Arapahos was mostly in blocks along the lower Canadian and North Canadian rivers. On April 19, 1892, the remainder of the reservation land was opened for homesteading. About thirty thousand settlers streamed onto the former reservation lands. The area was organized into six counties, and several towns were built. Now the Indians constituted only 10 percent of the population.

With Allotment came a new U.S. government effort to compel the Indians to assimilate, to adopt a style of life like that of their non-Indian neighbors. The *assimilation* policy assumed that if Indians were given very little economic assistance and forced to live on small family farms side by side with white farmers, they would see the superiority of their white neighbors' way of life and voluntarily change their own.

In 1895, the agent issued beef that had already been butchered to each head of household. This was an effort to undercut the authority of Arapaho leaders, who had previously held responsibility for distributing the beef ration to their followers. The agent ordered that no camps should contain more than four families, that the Arapahos were not to visit other families, that they were not to hold any assemblies or dances, Indian-custom marriages, or religious rituals, and they were not to share provisions. Failure to abide by these rules would result in a family's loss of rations or possibly a jail term. The Arapahos were stunned; the cession agreement that they had signed had promised rations and payments without setting any conditions.

To deflect the opposition of the Indian agents, Arapaho leaders adopted a strategy of placating them. The Cheyennes were openly resisting the agents' policies, so the Arapahos' apparent cooperation won them some concessions. Left Hand and other chiefs openly showed support for the schools and routinely visited them to encourage the students. In 1895, Left Hand consented to have a minister officiate at his daughter's marriage, which the agent believed set a good example for the other Indians. While the Cheyennes met resistance at every turn, Arapaho leaders convinced agents to permit their Offerings Lodge on several occasions. To get acceptance for the ceremony, they described it as an innocent-sounding "willow dance" on one occasion and a ceremony to pray for the crops at another. Later, during World War I, they would conceal the Offerings Lodge ceremony as a "patriotic dance" or a "Red Cross Dance." Embarrassed federal officials could hardly refuse the Arapaho permission to gather, ostensibly to raise money and pray for the war effort. They held other traditional dances under the guise of Christmas, Thanksgiving, or Fourth of July celebrations or as part of agricultural fairs.

Arapaho delegations like this one often traveled to Washington, D.C., to promote the rights of their people. In the latter part of the nineteenth century and early twentieth century, Arapahos were most concerned with obtaining more rations, more agency jobs for their people, protection of their land base, fair treatment by merchants, and religious freedom.

This strategy of accommodation rather than confrontation was designed to get other concessions from federal officials as well. On one occasion, in 1898, the Arapahos were allowed to send a delegation of chiefs to Washington, D.C., even though the Cheyennes were refused permission. The delegation succeeded in gaining more rations and more agency jobs for both the Cheyennes and the Arapahos. In later years, other delegations repeatedly pressured federal officials not to abolish the trust status of Indian-owned land, which would subject the already exploited people to taxation.

The loss of the reservation combined with the assimilation policy brought increased poverty to the Southern Arapahos and the Cheyennes. The problems encountered by the Northern Arapahos during the reservation era pale in comparison. In the

1890s the very lives of the Southern Arapahos were at risk, for some of their white neighbors felt no compunction about shooting Indians on sight. Between 1892 and 1901, the Southern Arapahos and Southern Cheyennes lost most of the property that they had managed to accumulate. Their white neighbors, many of whom had been poorer than the Indians when they arrived in 1892, trespassed on Indian allotments at will, stealing timber, tools, saddles, posts, wire, and, most significantly, livestock. Settlers who leased Indian land often stole the Indians' property and frequently failed to pay their rent. Crimes against Indians were ignored by territory officials. Gradually, the Indians became poorer and the whites more prosperous.

In the towns merchants prospered at the expense of the Indians. They loaned money to Indians at exorbitant interest rates, with property as collateral. When an Indian fell behind on repayments, the lenders seized property that was worth far more than the amount of the loan. The merchants charged Indians excessively high prices and encouraged them to buy on time. As soon as the Indians missed a payment, the merchants repossessed their merchandise.[30]

In the early twentieth century, it became obvious to federal officials that the measures intended to force assimilation had failed to eradicate Arapaho traditions. Harsher measures were instituted. Rations were stopped. Officials were determined that every man would farm or starve, but crop yields in this part of Oklahoma were too low to support even efficient, experienced white farmers on land similar to that of the Indians. The Arapahos had no choice but to depend on the small per-capita interest payment they received from the U.S. government and the money that they got from leasing the portion of their land that they could not farm. Officials, eager to gratify non-Indians clamoring for land, determined that leasing was a sign of laziness and started to encourage Indians to sell their land instead.

In 1902, Congress set aside the 1892 agreement and passed

the Dead Indian Land Act, which allowed Cheyenne and Arapaho heirs to sell the allotments they had inherited from deceased relatives. This was legally necessary in order to remove the land from the trust status provided for in the 1891 cession agreement. The 1902 act precipitated massive fraud; the agent was unable to protect the interests of the Indians, who generally were paid less than the land was worth.

In 1906, Congress passed the Burke Act, which allowed the secretary of the interior to declare Indians "competent" to receive a *fee patent*, or legal proof of ownership, on their allotment so that they could sell it. Again Indians were cheated. Persons incapable of understanding the transactions were not prevented from selling their land below market value. As historian Donald Berthrong has observed, even the U.S. government's own investigation—initiated after charges of corruption—concluded that the new legislation brought "joys to the grafter and confidence man and abject poverty to the Indian."[31]

Pressure from settlers for Indian land increased. Officials in Washington, D.C., responded in 1917 by declaring even more Arapahos and Cheyennes competent to manage their own affairs—and to sell their land. A fourth-grade education in a U.S. government vocational school was considered proof of competency. By 1920, more than half of the allotments had been sold; by 1928, 63 percent were no longer owned by Indians. Most families retained one member's land to live on or lease and gradually sold off the land of other family members.

The opening of the reservation resulted not only in the impoverishment of the Southern Arapahos; it also threatened their existence as a distinct community that had its own ways of maintaining order and organizing people to work together and help one another. The contrast with the Northern Arapahos is striking. Leaders in Wyoming were able to obtain greater control over tribal resources. As they gradually succeeded in this, they retained their people's respect. The

Southern Arapahos, on the other hand, had no tribal resources left, and so their leaders had little hope of improving the people's situation. By the 1930s, they were no longer able to provide for needy families. Because leadership was associated with generosity, the Southern Arapaho leaders gradually lost their people's confidence between 1892 and 1937.

The assimilation policies threatened to undermine the Arapahos' relationship with the Creator as well, for the agents attempted to prevent them from holding religious rituals. Chiefs were able, however, to prevent a ban on ceremonies, and they supported periodic gatherings that helped promote tribal unity and a sense of community.

Even after Allotment, Arapaho families still lived on the allotments of a band leader or a senior family member for a few months and in the large camps for the rest of the year. School-age children were sent away to the federal government boarding schools at Cantonment or Darlington. They were allowed to return to their families for Christmas, when the Arapahos gathered in one large camp (or, in the 1920s, two large camps, one near Canton and the other near Geary) and had dances and other entertainments. Children also returned to camp in the summer. In the fall, just before they went back to school, the tribe had a dance at which parents gave away what property they could—a blanket, a horse—to honor their children. In the twentieth century, the haircutting ritual had become unnecessary, because children and youths were used to having short hair; now the dance was the parents' way of preparing their children for school. Dances were also held during the two world wars for Arapaho soldiers.

Despite the assimilation policy, Arapahos of all ages retained a distinct cultural identity. Young people continued to marry with the customary exchange of gifts. Later, after the relationship appeared to be secure, a couple would also complete a legal ceremony. In-law avoidance and joking relationships persisted. Most married couples had to live on the allotment of a parent. By the 1920s, young people who had been born after the 1892 allotment process had no land of their own. Young men who had been trained in agricultural work at school helped their fathers or fathers-in-law farm. Those youths who had attended eastern boarding schools, such as Carlisle, had generally learned trades that they could not practice when they returned. Many worked at the agency as clerks or in some other capacity. Several of these youths, who formed a kind of elite group because they were better educated than most Arapahos, soon became disillusioned with the value of assimilating and returned to Arapaho traditional practices and beliefs. Some became regular participants in the Offerings Lodge, which continued to be vowed regularly until the early 1930s. Increasingly they became devotees of the peyote ritual, which had been introduced in the 1890s. By the 1920s, when they were of middle age, they were leaders in the peyote religion. Older leaders also relied on this group to serve as interpreters.

After receiving allotments, middle-aged men farmed a few acres, helping one another by sharing farm equipment and pooling their labor. In order to buy food and supplies for their families, they relied on credit extended by the stores in the area, which charged inflated prices. In exchange for supplies, the men put up their tools, farm equipment, livestock, and eventually their land as collateral. Sometimes they could not pay all of their bills and the merchants foreclosed. Women made a significant contribution to the income of the household with the money they received from leasing or selling their allotment lands. Federal regulations allowed women to inherit equally with their brothers, so a woman could own as much as or more land than the men in her family. By the 1920s, however, there was little land left to farm or lease.

By the 1920s, most Arapahos lived in houses. These were often built with the women's income and thus were considered the women's property, as the tepees had been. Families survived by community-wide sharing. Elders, who were likely to have inherited many allotments, were important contributors to the households of their children. People who helped the needy were held in high regard. Elders also put considerable time into fulfilling their ritual responsibilities.

There was much sickness. The scarcity and poor quality of food and shelter made people readily susceptible to contagious diseases. Tuberculosis was especially widespread. The Arapaho population continued to decline: In 1900 there had been 981 Southern Arapahos; in 1929, there were only 820.

In these times of adversity, the Arapahos relied on religion. At the turn of the twentieth century, virtually all Arapahos sought aid from the Creator through Offerings Lodge vows or other vows to sacrifice property to the Sacred Wheel. The Wheel was carried during the dancing in the Offerings Lodge by the individual who had vowed to sponsor the ceremony. Southern Arapahos often made prayer-sacrifices by donating property to the Wheel, as the Northern Arapahos in Wyoming did for the Sacred Pipe kept there. The Wheel, other articles used in the Offerings Lodge, and the Offerings Lodge itself symbolized the events of creation in Arapaho mythology. Each of the age-graded men's societies had a role in conducting the Offerings Lodge. Many men contributed time, money, and property, as society members and all men and women helped their relatives and friends to fulfill their ritual responsibilities. By the 1920s, those who had been middle-aged participants at the turn of the century were elders helping to direct the rite. In the 1920s, some young men participated; others were respectful but more committed to peyote ceremonies.

The peyote rite was introduced to the Southern Arapahos in the 1890s by individuals in the tribe who had participated in the peyote ceremonies of the Kiowa Indians. Participants stayed up all night fasting, singing religious songs, and praying while ingesting the peyote cactus, which has hallucinogenic properties, and following a ritual prescribed by the leader of the ceremony. Praying in the peyote ceremony was similar in many respects to more traditional ways of praying. Participants might receive a vision offering guidance and reassurance. The peyote served as a medium of prayer, as did the Sacred Pipe or Wheel. The peyote ritual served as a prayer-sacrifice, usually made to help someone recover from illness. Ceremonies were held after an individual vowed to the Creator to bear the expenses of the rite. The peyote rite allowed for a wide range of underlying beliefs and various interpretations of its symbols. Prayers could be made to the Great Mystery Above, God, the Creator, or Jesus Christ. Songs often focused on sacred birds as messengers to and from the supernatural world above; some participants believed that the birds were imbued with super-natural power; others thought that they symbolized angels.

In 1934, the Roosevelt administration began to sponsor legislation that made major reforms in federal Indian policy. The Oklahoma Indian Welfare Act was passed in 1937, and offi-cials assured the Cheyennes and the Arapahos that the remain-ing Indian-owned lands would remain in trust status indefinitely. Now officials pressured the Indians to approve a constitutional government and organize a business committee, whose members were to be tribally elected. Promises of eco-nomic aid and self-determination followed, but the hopes of Arapaho leaders were soon dashed because aid was minimal. Agricultural output declined. At the same time, the population increased, which was the result of a better health care system. The middle-aged leaders who were elected to the business council with the old chiefs' support were not able to demon-strate success to their followers in improving living conditions. The Arapahos did succeed in getting equal representation with the Cheyennes on the elected Cheyenne-Arapaho business committee, even though the Cheyennes still outnumbered the Arapahos two to one.

Economic decline and the advent of World War II caused many Arapahos to move to urban areas where they could find employment. Many sold their land. By 1951, two-thirds of the Cheyennes and the Arapahos were landless, and most of the rest owned only small fractional shares of the land that had been allotted to their deceased ancestors. Those in urban areas often returned to attend dances in the countryside, where the Arapahos retained campgrounds on a few remaining allotments, but few could make a living residing permanently on Arapaho lands.[32]

After the 1930s, Arapahos had to go to Wyoming to participate in the Offerings Lodge; there were no more elderly ritual authorities in Oklahoma. By the early 1960s, the Southern Arapahos had far more difficulty than the Northern division mobilizing tribal members to work for common goals, support tribal leaders, and participate in a tribal sharing network.

6

Arapahos and the War on Poverty

In the 1960s, public attitudes and federal government policies toward minorities changed. The struggles of civil rights activists to overcome discriminatory laws and customs led to greater tolerance for, and increased aid to, minority groups throughout the country. During the administrations of presidents John F. Kennedy and Lyndon B. Johnson, legislative programs known respectively as the New Frontier and the Great Society provided federal government financing for a variety of social programs. These included civil rights enforcement, an increase in educational opportunities, housing, job training, and economic development.

Indian reservations and communities were eligible for a number of these programs. As a result, the role of tribal governments expanded as their officials acquired new responsibilities and power. Tribal officials were involved in administering housing, public works, education, and other War on Poverty projects initiated by the

The Indian Self-Determination and Education Assistance Act of 1975 made it possible for the Northern Arapahos to take control of their children's education, which had previously been administered by the U.S. government. Shown here are two children who attend the Shoshone & Arapahoe Tribes Headstart program, located in Fort Washakie, Wyoming.

Johnson administration. In 1965, for example, the Department of Housing and Urban Development began an extensive program of building homes in Indian communities, and the Indian Health Service (a division of the Public Health Service) supported improvements in water supply and sanitation. The Elementary and Secondary Education Act of 1965 funded special programs for Indian students to increase their knowledge and appreciation of their cultural heritage.

Federal policy toward Indians in the 1970s centered on giving the tribal governments increased responsibility for administering government-funded programs. The Indian Self-Determination and Education Assistance Act of 1975 provided a means by which tribes could contract with the federal government to manage programs that had formerly been run by federal officials.

During the 1980s, the federal government did less for Indians; budget cuts terminated many government-related jobs and drastically reduced medical and other services to the needy. A general decline in oil prices also hurt the local economies of Wind River and Oklahoma. For the Northern Arapahos, the reservation and the community's commitment to helping one another were cushions against the economic reversals. The Southern Arapahos had less to fall back on.

From the late 1960s through the 1980s, Southern Arapaho families still lived on inherited allotments in the Oklahoma countryside, but many were clustered in tribal housing projects in Geary or lived in private homes in towns. At least half of the Southern Arapahos lived outside the area that was originally allotted to the Arapahos. Very little land was still Indian-owned—only about 77,000 acres out of the half-million allotted in 1892. Many older Arapahos owned shares in the allotments of ancestors, and they received a percentage of rental fees and royalties for oil and gas produced on their land. This income was small and unequally distributed among the population, but it allowed elderly people to continue making an important economic contribution to the subsistence of their households.[33]

Subagencies and the U.S. government boarding schools closed from the late 1920s through the 1970s. Tribal officials succeeded in having the lands on which they were situated, some ten thousand acres, revert to the tribes. This tribally held property then was leased for farming, grazing, and mineral development. Income from farming and grazing leases—about $130,000 a year—paid for the tribal government's operating expenses and supported some programs to alleviate the poverty of tribal members. Most of the oil and gas royalties from the tribally owned land were distributed on a per-person basis once a year to the members of the Southern Cheyenne and the Southern Arapaho tribes. The payment was a small one.[34]

Most of the Oklahoma Arapahos lived in poverty. Unemployment ranged from 40 to 70 percent (compared with a national unemployment rate of 5 to 15 percent). There were not enough jobs locally, and Indians often faced discrimination when they applied for jobs in the non-Indian world. Families got some income from employment and services subsidized by the federal government, when the tribal government con-tracted to operate programs such as Child Welfare and Indian Health. Many tribal members received additional income in the form of public assistance, social security, or military pensions directly from state and federal sources.

In 1975, the tribes revised the 1937 constitution. Thereafter, the Southern Arapaho communities in the Geary and Canton areas each elected two members to represent them on the Cheyenne-Arapaho Business Committee. Four other elected members represented the four Cheyenne communities. Tribal members who lived outside the Geary and Canton communities could be very influential in these elections and also could be candidates for these positions. Adult tribal members, that is, all those who had one-fourth Cheyenne and/or Arapaho ancestry and one parent enrolled in the Cheyenne-Arapaho tribes, voted. Since 1966, women have been elected to the committee. Committee members, who received salaries after the tribes began to contract programs, supervised federally funded pro-grams and served as advocates for the people in their relations with oil companies, local and state officials, and the federal gov-ernment. They instituted tribally owned businesses, including a bingo operation at Concho, the site of the tribal offices. The committee's job has been particularly difficult because its constituency includes Cheyennes and Arapahos who live outside the Indian community and who resent receiving fewer services than community people. The new constitution also allowed tribal members who attend an annual meeting to vote on the tribes' budget.[35]

Business committee members generally were middle-aged. Elders continued to be respected, but those in Oklahoma had less influence than their Northern Arapaho counterparts, because the center of Arapaho religious ritual is in Wyoming. Young people had greater independence than they formerly did. The tribes used tribal income to set up a scholarship fund for higher education. Many young men and women earned college degrees and then attempted to obtain jobs working for the tribes in managerial positions; others chose to seek wage work in urban areas throughout Oklahoma or elsewhere. The children began to attend public schools, where they were a minority. They learned their place in Arapaho society through family life and by participating in benefit dances and other community activities.[36]

Life in the Geary and Canton Arapaho communities revolved (and still resolves), to a great extent, around the benefit dances. These were held almost every weekend. Arapaho living elsewhere returned to attend the dances, which raised money for many causes, from helping needy individuals to aiding service clubs, to covering the expenses of summer *powwows*, or gatherings.

Families or organizations usually sponsored dances and powwows. Planning for a benefit dance began many weeks in advance. The sponsor first chose at least seven people to serve as head staff—a head singer, head male and female dancers, young boy and girl dancers, a master of ceremonies, and an arena director. The head singer took responsibility for gathering a drum group together to sing at the dance. Head dancers led the dancing and urged others to join in. The master of ceremonies presided over the event, instructed people on procedure, and commented on the activity. Finally, the arena director made sure the hall or grounds where the dance was to be held were ready, and helped carry the food and gifts that were exchanged at the dance. These positions were modern counterparts of older ones; the master of ceremonies, for example, was equivalent to the camp crier of earlier days who announced to the people the consensus-based decisions of the elders.

The entire family of every member of the head staff was expected to help collect the gifts and food to be given away at the dance. The sponsor arranged for food to be cooked and also obtained gifts for the *giveaway*, which was held before the main events of the dance began. Every person on the head staff gave gifts to each of the others, so several hours were needed for all the gifts to be presented. The head singer, for example, gave at least a blanket to each of the other men, a shawl to each of the women, and a basket of groceries to each of the children on the head staff. After the gifts were presented, a special dance honored the sponsoring family that gave gifts. The people in attendance joined in the dance and then contributed money to the sponsoring family, which donated the money to the evening's cause. Gift exchanges helped to maintain the sense of mutual obligation and goodwill that were essential to the continuation of these rituals. During the dance, the master of ceremonies called for dances to honor a category of people, such as veterans or people from a particular area; members of the category so honored were obligated to dance and also contribute money to the evening's cause.

Most Southern Arapaho families were involved as sponsors or head staff members in at least one benefit dance a year. Leaders, such as elected officials, and people who are employed, especially those who work for the tribe, were expected to participate frequently.

(*continued on page 108*)

Powwow Dancing

Several distinct kinds of dance styles and associated songs are common at the powwows in Arapaho and Cheyenne country. The dance styles bring to mind the movements of animals and other forces of nature. The "gourd dance" is held in the early afternoon before the contest dancing begins. In this type of song, the drum has a loud-soft beat. Men dance in a line in unison and bounce slightly on their heels while standing in place and shaking gourd rattles (or tin cans with pebbles or shot) in time to the song. After the song is sung once or twice, the beat gets louder and the excitement builds. At the end of the song, there is a flurry of fast beats, and the dancers shake their rattles. Women dance in place around the periphery of the arena. The men carry fans and wear street clothes, a beaded bandoleer with a silk scarf over the left shoulder, a red and blue woolen shoulder blanket around the neck, and a long sash with beaded and fringed ends around the waist.

There are four kinds of war dances used for men's contest dancing. In the war dance, the drum beat is even and unaccented except at certain transition points in the song. These are free and individualistic dance styles, but each participant has a distinct kind of outfit and movement. Attitude is an important part of style. Young men usually are "fancy" and "grass" dancers. The fancy dancer emphasizes footwork and speed: spinning, doing kneefalls, and abruptly changing posture. His outfit includes matching feather bustles at his neck and back. The back bustle attaches to a beaded belt. Some of these bustles open and shut like wings with the movements of the dancer. The dancer wears a feathered roach, beaded headband, beaded front and back apron, fringed cape or ribbon shirt, beaded cuffs and armbands or feathered arm-wheels, a beaded shoulder harness, bells at the knees, anklets of white Angora fur, and moccasins.

The grass dancer emphasizes the upper body and footwork, shaking his shoulders, swaying from side to side, darting quickly, and changing directions. He wears no bustle but, rather, fringed cloth pants, an apron with long ribbons hanging from it, fringed shirt, beaded belt, cuffs, armbands, head harness, shoulder harness, headband with a roach made from automobile choke cables, bells, Angora anklets, and moccasins. As the dancer moves, the long ribbons suggest the movement of prairie grass.

Older men usually are "traditional" or "straight" dancers. The traditional dancer uses free-style steps, specialized facial expressions, and head and shoulder movements that suggest the movement of birds. He wears a hair roach headdress of porcupine quills or sisal fiber that imitates the crests on birds, one feathered bustle patterned after a bird's spreading tail feathers, arm wheels of feathers that suggest wings, a beaded front and back apron, and moccasins. The straight dancer is restrained and dignified with an erect posture. He uses a walking step. He wears cloth tailored pants and a shirt with two trailers hanging from his neck and back, a roach headdress with a feather, a silk kerchief, a bandoleer, an apron and beaded belt, and moccasins.

Women have four war dance styles for contest dancing. The "buckskin dress" dancer does a dignified walking step and wears a beaded buckskin dress with fringe almost to the ground, beaded leggings and moccasins, and beaded hair ties. The "cloth dress" dancer also does a walking step. Her dress is made of broadcloth, silk, or cotton and it reaches mid-calf and often is decorated with shells. She wears beaded leggings and moccasins. Young women usually are "fancy shawl" and "jingle dress" dancers. The fancy shawl dancer uses very fast and elaborate footwork. She spins and uses her elaborately decorated shawl to accentuate upper-body movement. She wears a satin dress just below or at the knee, beaded leggings, and moccasins. The jingle dress dancer uses fast hopping steps. Her cloth dress is mid-calf length and is covered with horizontal rows of "jingles" made of the lids of snuff cans that clink when she moves. She also wears leggings and moccasins.

In addition to the dance styles used in contest dancing, there are other social dances, such as the "round dance," in which both men and women form a circle and dance around the arena in a side-step. The "two-step" is a dance for a man and woman dancing as a couple. Gourd and war dancing also occur outside of the context of contests and anyone in the crowd can participate.*

* Information adapted from William K. Powers, *War Dance: Plains Indian Musical Performance* (Tucson, Ariz.: University of Arizona, 1980).

(*continued from page 105*)

Some of the money raised in benefit dances went to sponsor summer powwows, which tribal members traveled hundreds of miles to attend. The Geary Arapahos sponsored a powwow in July, and the Canton Arapahos held one in August. An even larger powwow followed in September sponsored by both the Southern Arapahos and the Southern Cheyennes.

At the powwows, veterans, various leaders, and elders were recognized and honored by the community. Noted dancers from many different tribes entered contests and competed for cash prizes. Because dances were once forbidden, their persistence symbolized to the Arapahos their success in resisting exploitation and victimization by the federal government and non-Indians. The survival and contemporary elaboration of the dancing tradition was and is perceived as a hard-won victory.[37]

Peyote ceremonies continued to be a focus of spiritual life, drawing together Arapahos from Geary and Canton and more distant towns, as well as people from other tribes. Participants may vow to sponsor (that is, pay the expenses of) a peyote ceremony as a prayer-sacrifice. The peyote religion is known as the Native American Church. The supernatural help sought may be in the form of a cure, a child's health and success in life, or other kinds of assistance. Many Arapahos also attended Christian churches, primarily of Protestant faiths. But the most important ritual for many Arapahos remained the Offerings Lodge, held every summer at Wind River in Wyoming. Southern Arapahos traveled there regularly to participate in this ceremony held by the Northern Arapahos. Some of the money raised through benefit dances during the year paid for travel expenses and ritual obligations. In recent years, an increasing number of Southern Arapahos have been going to Wyoming to celebrate the Offerings Lodge. Like powwows, the Offerings Lodge has brought all Arapahos together to express their commitment to the Arapaho community and identity.[38]

Although the two divisions visited, communicated, and

The Wind River Reservation lies fifteen miles northwest of Lander, Wyoming, in Fremont County. The 118,000 acres of wilderness contains 265 lakes and 1,164 miles of streams and rivers, and is bordered on three sides by mountain ranges.

shared the Arapaho identity, they continued to have different experiences. The four thousand Northern Arapahos remained centered on Wind River Reservation, largely residing on allotments. In the mid-1960s most of them were living in mobile homes or small log or frame houses, often without plumbing and electricity. Since then, new or remodeled frame or prefabricated homes, ranch style or split-level, have been built on most of the allotments, and two housing projects were built through federally funded programs.[39]

Wind River Reservation is fifty-five miles long and seventy miles wide—largely wide-open space. Very few non-Indians resided on the reservation, and those who did avoided contact with the Indians. The Arapahos did their shopping in Lander and Riverton, towns that border the reservation, but had little personal contact with the residents of the towns.

During the 1960s and 1970s, Northern Arapaho children grew up in extended family settlements. These consisted of several houses clustered together, with the grandparents' household at the spiritual and social center. Because parents often worked, grandparents or older siblings usually watched the small children during the day. Adults accepted responsibility for caring for the children of their brothers and sisters. Children had many grandparents, because they called the brothers and sisters of their grandparents by the same terms as they used for their actual grandmother and grandfather. Children could live for a time in the household of one relative, then in that of another. When old enough to help elders, children might live with their grandparents. Thus, child care was widely shared. Children learned to be unobtrusive in their relations with others, to repress anger, to defer to elders, to be generous with possessions, and to persuade rather than demand.

During the summer, children rode the family's horses and played with their cousins—whom they knew as "brothers" and "sisters." They attended public school on the reservation during the remainder of the year. Few non-Indian children attended these schools, and Arapaho parents had influence over school policies. Arapaho language and culture, particularly stories and handcrafts, were taught there. In 1972 and 1976 organized groups of parents contracted with the federal government to operate two high schools so that Arapaho children could complete secondary school on the reservation in an environment that affirmed tribal values.

For teenagers, sports were (and still are) a major preoccupation and a source of community pride; Indian high school teams played, often quite successfully, against their counterparts from Wyoming's non-Indian communities. After graduating from high school, some young people went on to college, while many joined the armed services or sought employment on the reservation. But there were not enough jobs on the reservation, and unemployment became even more of a serious problem when the federal government cut spending on federal programs in the 1980s.

The Wind River Reservation lies at the foothills of Wyoming's Rocky Mountains and is home to both the Shoshones and Northern Arapahos. The reservation is fifty-five miles long and seventy miles wide, and is largely composed of wide-open space. Shown here is a home on the reservation near Lander.

Until a young man reached his thirties, older Arapahos did not consider him stable or settled and he had only a limited role in community activities. Young men joined some clubs, sometimes in the capacity of helpers or apprentices. Girls assisted their mothers in their club activities. Young men and women increasingly married while still in their teens, even before they found employment. Some newly married couples began married life in housing projects, but they still spent much of their time at their parents' and grandparents' homes.

Mature men and women attempted to find work on the reservation. Most job openings were in tribal government projects, but these were limited. Even at the peak of President Johnson's War on Poverty programs, unemployment among the Wind River Arapahos was 48 percent. Those who did have jobs helped support relatives who were unemployed. Outside of work, much time was spent helping with activities of the clubs, such as the Christmas and Memorial clubs, and those who aspired to leadership positions in the community were particularly diligent about donating time and money.[40]

Every fall, the local American Legion posts and associated Women's Auxiliaries sponsored a Veterans' Day dance. These two posts, located on the reservation at Ethete and Arapahoe, were composed primarily of Arapaho veterans of World War II, although younger veterans sometimes joined as well. They also conducted flag ceremonies at events throughout the year and organized military funerals. In the winter, the Christmas Club sponsored a week of dancing and other activities. The Memorial Club assumed responsibility for a yearly spring dance and for maintaining and decorating graves. Two committees organized the summer pow-wows that are attended by tribes from all over the plains. People come to camp, visit, and participate in games and dance contests at the two powwows. Women had an important role in all these events; they not only prepared the food for communal feasts but also took responsibility for give-away ceremonies. At powwow giveaways, families honored relatives by giving away property (such as quilts, shawls, kitchen utensils, and clothing) to others.

An elected six-member business council continued to work with the Shoshone Business Council to manage Wind River's lands and resources. The council decided who could lease tribal land (and gave preference to Indians) and purchased land from individuals who wished to sell their allotments. Most reservation land was (and still is) held in trust; 78 percent was tribally owned, and most of the remainder of the reservation's nearly 2.5 million acres was owned by individual Arapahos. The Northern Arapaho Business Council instituted several tribally owned businesses, including a gas station and two grocery stores; the tribe also has owned a cattle ranch since 1940 (see sidebar on pages 72–73).[41]

In the late 1970s, oil and gas royalties and bonuses from tribal lands brought the Northern Arapahos $4.5 million each year. Eighty-five percent of this was distributed in per-person payments; out of the remainder, the business council was given a budget of about $400,000 to administer, in addition to monies received from federal programs. It used some of this money, plus loans from the federal government, to buy—and thus keep in the tribe—land from Arapahos and from non-Indians.

Much of the Northern Arapahos' budget supported the activities of the clubs and paid for essentials—such as groceries, necessary travel, school supplies, and funeral costs—for needy individuals. The council gave hiring preference to those who were most in need. The council sought to pressure the federal government into assuming greater financial responsibility for the reservation. Its members believed and continue to assert that financial support is a federal obligation resulting from the treaty relationship between the Northern Arapahos and the U.S. government.[42]

Every two years, the Northern Arapahos elected an entertainment committee whose six members coordinated and supervised community celebrations and oversaw the spending of money allocated to clubs. The members of both the business council and entertainment committee were generally leaders in secular concerns, whereas elders retained authority in religious matters.

Elders continued to try to influence the tribe's goals and to mobilize community support for these goals and for the business council. The custom was for a general council of tribal members to set policy. In the general council meetings the elders tried to shape opinion. The elders' control gradually lessened after 1972, when younger Arapahos successfully pressed the general council to establish a primary election for the business council. Elders no longer could nominate candidates from the floor. In 1981, younger Shoshone and Arapaho tribal members discovered that oil companies were underreporting the quantity of oil they shipped off the reservation. This scandal propelled younger, formally educated Arapahos into business council politics. Younger people were elected to the committee, although voters also chose one or two older, experienced men. Only one woman, Nellie Scott, served on the council during the 1960s through the 1980s.[43]

A group of elderly men and women continued to supervise sacred ceremonies at Wind River. One of these ritual leaders took care of the Sacred Pipe and presided over its rites. The Pipe contained, and reminded the Arapahos of, the supernatural power available to them if they as a tribal group continued to cooperate with one another, act in harmony, and fulfill their ritual responsibilities. The Pipe remains central to Arapaho religious life today.[44]

The Offerings Lodge remained the most important religious ceremony involving the entire community. In July, all Northern Arapaho families—and many Southern Arapaho families—camp for seven days at Wind River. Individuals who have vowed to do so make the prayer-sacrifice in the lodge. The participants' families prepare food that is exchanged throughout the entire camp, thus symbolizing tribal unity. Everyone attempts to concentrate on the sacred occasion and avoid any social conflict. In the lodge, the story of creation is dramatized, and participants, old and young, male and female, fulfill their vows to the Creator through prayer and fasting. In recent years, the Arapahos have devoted an increasing amount of money and effort to this ceremony. Many Indians from other tribes travel hundreds of miles to be present at the event.

Formally educated youths as well as older Arapahos continue to seek their place in Arapaho society through family life and participation in the Offerings Lodge.

7

Northern and Southern Arapahos Today

Today, approximately 7,347 Arapahos and Cheyennes live in the area in west-central Oklahoma that was once their reservation. Thanks in large part to Public Law 638 (the Self-Determination Act), which was passed by Congress in 1975, the Arapahos, in cooperation with the Cheyennes, have been able to contract most of the programs that were formerly administered by the federal and state governments so that they now can employ more tribal members and operate the programs more in keeping with traditional values. For example, child-welfare workers use traditional ideas of "family" when they select foster parents. Arapaho children might be placed with "grandparents," "aunts and uncles," or "mothers" and "fathers"—people who were siblings or cousins of biological relatives. The tribes use their own standards, rather than those of the state, in setting economic requirements for fostering children. In this way, they help children retain close ties to their heritage.

Clara Bushyhead, a spokesperson for the Southern Cheyenne and Arapaho tribes, speaks at a 2004 news conference. Behind her is the flag of the two tribes, which includes two sets of fourteen eagle feathers and fourteen stars—each representing the fourteen members of the old tribal council.

The tribes established several businesses that employ tribal members—more bingo halls, more cigarette and sundry shops, and gas stations. They purchased interests in the oil wells on tribal land and they entered an agreement with a management company to operate Lucky Star Casino at Concho, Oklahoma. They also expanded the Farm and Ranch business.

The Cheyenne-Arapaho Business Committee tries to create as many jobs as possible; nonetheless, unemployment stands at 40 percent. Twenty-two percent of the families have income below the poverty level, which is considerably higher than the percentage for non-Indians. Some Arapahos and Cheyennes chose to work in Oklahoma City (about twenty minutes from tribal headquarters) and its environs; so the economic circumstances of Southern Arapahos are better than those of the Northern Arapahos. In Wyoming, a very rural area, 36 percent of Arapaho families live below the poverty level and the median and per-capita income are significantly below the income of Southern Arapahos.

The Cheyenne-Arapaho tribes operate their own educational programs from federal funds and from a large tribal educational trust established after they received a settlement in 1961 from a suit filed against the United States. The suit requested damages for settlers trespassing on Arapaho and Cheyenne lands that were reserved to them in the Fort Laramie Treaty of 1851. College and graduate students and tribal members in law and medical schools receive assistance from the tribes. The tribes' education department has used federal funds to offer Arapaho and Cheyenne language classes to the public.[45]

The percentage of Southern and Northern Arapahos who have earned their high school diploma is about the same, 79 percent to 75 percent. In terms of higher education, 12 percent of Arapahos and Cheyennes have a bachelor's degree or higher, compared to 5 percent of Northern Arapahos. The Oklahoma tribes dedicated themselves to improving higher education in the late 1960s, which may account for the difference. There are two community colleges and two state universities in Cheyenne and Arapaho country.[46]

The State of Oklahoma objected to many of the tribes' efforts to promote economic development. A plan to expand Lucky Star Casino to offer table games and video machines met state resistance and therefore was thwarted, because Congress had mandated that the tribes make gaming agreements with states for the most lucrative games. Since the tribes won a court case against them in 1997, the oil companies have had to pay the tribes a tax on oil removed from tribal land, and since 1996 the tribes have issued license plates on which they collect a tax. Taxes collected from businesses that operate on tribal land are used for law enforcement and other services, as well as emergency assistance for needy families. The best chance the tribes have for economic development is to recover land held in reserve by the federal government at the former site of Fort Reno. Other reservation land (10,400 acres) has been restored to tribal ownership and is currently used for sites for tribal businesses and program offices. This reservation land was not ceded in 1892 but, instead, it was used by the federal government. Fort Reno has long been vacated by the U.S. Army and the acreage is adjacent to Interstate 40 and would be an excellent location for businesses. However, the state's congressional representatives and local officials have successfully blocked the return of Fort Reno land to the tribes.[47]

Despite the tribal leaders' success in the legal conflicts over taxation and in the development of businesses and contracting of programs, many constituents have expressed dissatisfaction with the elected Cheyenne-Arapaho Business Committee. As is the case for many tribal governments, the dissatisfaction is caused, first, by high expectations that cannot be met by the available jobs, scholarships, housing, and services. Second, elected officials are paid salaries from the overhead costs associated with programs, so constituents may view officials as profiting personally from program funds and resent them for it. Third, bureaucratic red tape associated with programs makes accounting for program funds difficult, and these problems work against the business committee members' efforts to convince their constituents that they are good managers.[48]

The new emphasis on tribal sovereignty has buttressed and been strengthened by the Arapahos' continued commitment to dances and powwows. The Arapahos installed several new honorary chiefs, whose job is to support traditional activities and values. They and their wives participate in and sponsor dances and are involved in the Offerings Lodge in Wyoming or the Native American Church, or both. Women play an important part in the giveaway ceremonies that are associated with tribal

The Arapahos are one of more than twenty Native American tribes who consider Devil's Tower sacred. The monolith, located in northeastern Wyoming, is known as "Bear's Tipi," and now plays an important role in Arapaho culture, along with the Medicine Wheel, which is located in Wyoming's Bighorn National Forest.

ceremonies. The authorization of a National Park Service historic site at the location of the Sand Creek Massacre in November 2000 and at the sacred Medicine Wheel site (a stone monument in Wyoming) also has reinforced interest in traditional activities and contributed to pride in Arapaho identity. The Medicine Wheel, located in the Bighorn National Forest in Bighorn County is a circle of rocks enclosing twenty-eight radial rows of rock extending from a cairn in the center. It is seventy-five feet in diameter. The site is at an elevation of 9,642 feet and is part of a complex of interrelated sites that have been used by Native people for approximately seven thousand years. The builder(s) of the wheel in Bighorn County is unknown. There are between 70 and 150 medicine wheel sites in South Dakota, Wyoming, Montana, Alberta, and Saskatchewan. Today, Native people, including the Arapahos, use the Medicine Wheel site for prayer ceremonies. There is a ceremonial staging area, a sweat lodge site, an altar, and places to make offerings and fast for visions. Native people also gather medicinal and ceremonial plants in the area.[49]

In the 1990s, the Northern Arapahos faced opposition from the State of Wyoming as they tried to exercise the rights recognized by Congress and the federal courts. Even though courts had ruled that services should be provided to the reservation with taxes collected by the state on oil and gas produced on tribal land, state officials ignored the needs of reservation residents. The Arapaho tribe's effort to start casino gambling was blocked by the state. The Arapahos and Shoshone tribes have also encountered resistance from the state because they have their own fish and game department that enforces tribal codes. The tribes had attempted to build up depleted herds of game animals and apply traditional values to hunting and fishing activity, such as issuing permits to individuals to hunt not only for themselves but also for widows, elders, and disabled persons. State fish and game wardens declined to honor the tribes' regulations within the reservation boundaries. County and state courts refused to accept the jurisdiction of the tribal court, despite federal rulings. Water rights, however, was the issue that most preoccupied the tribes and the state.[50]

The Wind River Reservation was established by a treaty the Shoshones signed with the U.S. government in 1868. The treaty guaranteed that the reservation would be a homeland where the Shoshones could farm, hunt, and fish. Later, in 1904, when the Arapahos were occupants of the reservation, the U.S. government pressured the Shoshones and Arapahos to cede the northern half of the reservation with a promise that an irrigation system would be built for them on the southern half of the reservation. Those lands were not supposed to be taxed or sold. Instead, the federal government allowed settlers to purchase land on the reservation, as well as on the ceded portion, and money appropriated for the Arapahos and Shoshones paid for an irrigation system used by non-Indians. Indian farming took a backseat to federal support for non-Indian farmers, who benefited from many forms of exploitation of the tribes.[51]

The reservation contains 118,000 acres of wilderness with 265 lakes and 1,164 miles of streams and rivers that rise in the mountains on the west side of the reservation. Hunting and fishing play a minimal role in subsistence today, but the Arapahos and Shoshones feel a strong connection to the wilderness area and the wildlife there. The obligation to protect wildlife is a religious duty and a means of respecting the sacrifices of their ancestors who fought for the right of survival of subsequent generations. The irrigation projects serving non-Indians have gradually destroyed trout fisheries and undermined Arapaho and Shoshone agricultural development. In 1977, the tribes contested the state's control of the water on the reservation when the state argued that the tribes had no water rights at all. Tribal leaders were determined to promote fisheries and Indian agriculture. Sports fishing could be developed to provide income for the tribes, to create jobs for tribal members, and to preserve the wilderness area. A long legal battle ensued, culminating in a Supreme Court decision in 1989, which stated that the tribes had an 1868 treaty-right to more than half the water from the Wind River Basin. State

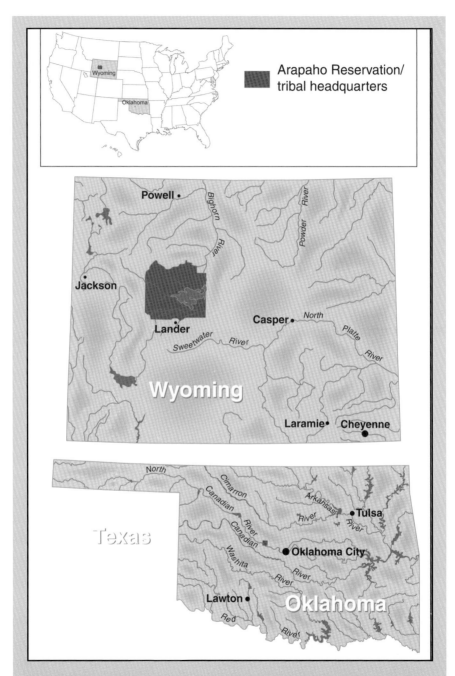

The Wind River Reservation, located in west-central Wyoming, is today home to the Shoshone and Northern Arapaho people. The Shoshones and Northern Arapahos own 1.8 of the 2.2-million-acre reservation. The tribal headquarters of the Southern Arapahos and Southern Cheyennes lies just to the west of Oklahoma City, Oklahoma.

officials subsequently refused to cooperate with the tribes and continued to divert water from fisheries and Indian farms to about six hundred non-Indian operators of small family ranches. These small ranches are gradually decreasing as land is purchased by non-local people for summer homes. The economic problems of six thousand Arapahos and Shoshones remain unaddressed.[52]

Poverty on the reservation is a major problem. Oil and gas revenues declined in the 1990s due to falling prices, so the tribes had less money to help those in need, and the per-capita payments to tribal members declined to as low as $40 a month. Tribal leaders contracted health, education, and economic programs from the federal and state governments. Because the program money was evenly divided between Shoshones and Arapahos and the Arapaho population on the reservation (3,810 in 1999) was more than double that of the Shoshones, the Northern Arapaho Business Council moved its offices to Ethete and began to contract programs independently of the Shoshones. The business council employs tribal members in the programs and in tribally owned businesses, including grocery stores, bingo, gas stations, a construction company, a farming enterprise, and the Arapahoe Ranch, which is self-supporting and one of the largest in the state.[53]

The business council, supported by the Northern Arapaho General Council, provided the leadership in the fight for water rights. Beginning in the 1980s, young college-educated Arapahos took prominent roles in pursuing more tribal control over reservation life and resources. The general council supported this more aggressive stance. College-educated women began to run for tribal offices and two were elected between 1990 and 1994. The general council created the Northern Arapaho Economic Development Commission to try to generate more business opportunity and the Northern Arapaho Trust to manage tribal businesses. Some women won election to the former, and a few elders were appointed to the Northern

Arapaho Trust. Generally, these new organizations provided more positions of authority for younger Arapahos. As in Oklahoma, the large sums of money obtained through tribal contracts and a settlement from oil companies raised expectations, yet the amount of money was not adequate to relieve unemployment and poverty. Competition for these monies undermined the constituents' trust of tribal officials, as did the lack of success in the struggle to enforce water rights.[54]

Another controversy centered on the criteria for enrollment in the tribe. A group of women, some unmarried and others married to non-Arapaho men, petitioned the general council to enroll their children. For several years, the general council insisted that to be enrolled a child must have an enrolled Arapaho father and at least one-fourth Arapaho ancestry, and that the child's parents must be married. In 1985, the council created an associate membership category for the children who had one-fourth Arapaho ancestry and an enrolled mother rather than father. The associate members could benefit from programs but could not vote, receive the per-capita payment, or hold office on the reservation. This change followed the realization that the *Indian Child Welfare Act* only applied to enrolled children and that nonenrolled children would be "lost" to the tribe through adoption by non-Indians. In 1992, the women advocating change reintroduced the matter to the general council, which subsequently voted to enroll these children, who numbered more than seven hundred. Unlike in earlier times, general councils became contentious, and elderly people's authority became more narrow in scope.[55]

Elders remain the authorities on religious matters, including the Offerings Lodge, and the Four Old Men—who now serve as religious leaders for the tribe—play a major role in helping the Arapaho community cope with serious social problems. They hold "days of healing" during which they perform rituals to restore the health of the community and provide psychological support for Arapahos; for example, when there is violent conflict among them.

The 1990s brought a dramatic increase in juvenile crime and drug abuse. One contributing factor was the construction of new housing projects where young parents with children lived apart from older relatives. Also, unlike in earlier times, many youths are products of marriages where only one parent is Arapaho. On the reservation, there is a smaller pool of relatives who can counsel and care for these children in the many instances where the non-Arapaho parent is from another reservation or tribal community. Also, non-Arapaho relatives often live according to a value system different from that of the Arapahos. Media and other influences from the non-Indian world shape children's attitudes. The strong Arapaho extended family that works to socialize children to conform to Arapaho values faces these and other challenges. To help youths develop constructive life goals, elders took the lead in prioritizing higher education, and their support resulted in the general council's decision to invest $500,000 in scholarship money that was matched by the University of Wyoming. More than forty Arapahos have graduated from the university. In 1997, students began enrolling in Wind River Tribal College at Ethete, Wyoming. Elders also obtained money from the general council to start summer language and culture camps for children in an attempt to reverse the trend toward children growing up without training in Arapaho values. The business council has made it a priority to create programs for youths, and elders have been given important roles in these programs, where they introduce traditional ways of healing and changing behavior.[56]

Through Arapaho determination and commitment, the language, values, and other aspects of Northern Arapaho life that the non-Indian society once tried to eradicate, have endured. Today, Arapaho culture remains a source of strength and fulfillment for the Arapaho people of Oklahoma as well as those of Wyoming.

The Arapahos at a Glance

Tribe	Arapaho
Culture Area	Great Plains
Geography	At contact, the northern plains; from the mid-nineteenth century, Northern Arapahos on the plains of southern Wyoming and northern Colorado; Southern Arapahos on the plains of west-central Oklahoma and southern Kansas
Linguistic Family	Algonquian
Current Population	Approximately 11,000*
First European Contact	Jean Baptiste Trudeau, French, 1795
Federal Status	Recognized; Wind River Reservation in Wyoming is the Northern Arapaho tribal land; Southern Arapahos have no reservation but own tribal land

* Includes combined population of Southern Cheyennes and Southern Arapahos.

1730   Arapahos acquire horses about this time.

1772   English trader Matthew Cocking makes first recorded European contact with Gros Ventre division of Arapahos.

1795   Jean Baptiste Trudeau makes first recorded European contact with Northern and Southern Arapahos.

1805   Arapahos make a formal peace and trade agreement with Spanish in Santa Fe, New Mexico.

1835   Arapahos make a treaty of peace with U.S. Colonel Henry Dodge and the United States.

1851   Northern and Southern Arapahos sign the Fort Laramie Treaty agreeing to allow settlers to pass through their territory.

1861   Southern Arapahos sign a treaty agreeing to cede land.

1864   Arapahos killed at Sand Creek Massacre in Colorado and as a result the Arapahos are drawn into war with the United States.

1865   Northern Arapahos join Cheyennes and Sioux in war against United States over Powder River country.

1867   Southern Arapahos sign Medicine Lodge Creek treaty agreeing to settle on a reservation.

1868   Northern Arapahos sign Fort Laramie Treaty agreeing to settle on a reservation.

1869   President Ulysses S. Grant creates a reservation for Southern Arapahos and Southern Cheyennes on Canadian River and Arapahos settle there in 1870 (in what is now Oklahoma).

1874   Northern Arapahos are attacked in Wyoming by U.S. troops (Bates Battle).

1878   Northern Arapahos settle on Shoshone Reservation in Wyoming.

1889–90   Northern and Southern Arapahos embrace the Ghost Dance.

1892   Southern Arapahos receive allotments and the reservation is opened for settlement.

1896   Northern Arapahos agree to cede part of the Shoshone Reservation.

1900	Northern Arapahos receive allotments on the Shoshone Reservation.
1905	Northern Arapahos agree to a cession of the northern half of the Shoshone Reservation.
1906	Burke Act passed by Congress allows subsequent sale of some Arapaho allotments in Wyoming and many in Oklahoma.
1935	Northern Arapahos reject the Indian Reorganization Act and refuse to organize a constitutional government.
1936	Southern Arapahos accept the provisions of the Oklahoma Indian Welfare Act and organize a constitutional government with the Cheyennes.
1941–45	Arapahos join the U.S. armed forces and work in war industry during World War II.
1947	Northern Arapahos get congressional consent for their oil royalties to be paid in person-to-person payments.
1955	The Indian Claims Commission rules the United States violated the 1851 treaty with the Arapahos and Cheyennes.
1961	Northern and Southern Arapahos win monetary settlement against the United States for the violation of the 1851 treaty.
1967–69	War on Poverty programs begin among Northern and Southern Arapahos.
1972	Northern Arapahos open a contract high school.
1975	Indian Self-Determination and Education Assistance Act passed by Congress and subsequently Arapahos begin contracting programs.
1988	Tribal courts established by Cheyenne-Arapaho and Wind River tribes.
1989	Supreme Court rules Northern Arapahos and Shoshones have 1868 treaty right to more than half the water on the Wind River Reservation.
1997	Southern Arapahos and Cheyennes win case in tribal supreme court against oil companies, which obligates companies to pay tribes a tax on oil recovered from tribal lands; Northern Arapahos open Wind River Tribal College.

NOTES

Chapter 1:
Devotees and Prophets

1   George A. Dorsey, and Alfred L. Kroeber, *Traditions of the Arapaho*, Field Columbian Museum Anthropological Series 5, 1903, 1–6; see also Fowler 1982, 108.

2   James Mooney, *The Ghost-Dance Religion and the Sioux Outbreak of 1890*, Fourteenth Annual Report of the Bureau of American Ethnology (Washington, D.C., 1896), 775.

3   Dorsey and Kroeber, *Traditions of the Arapaho*, 7–8.

4   See John C. Ewers, *The Horse in Blackfoot Indian Culture with Comparative Material from Other Western Tribes* (Washington, D.C.: Smithsonian Institution Press, 1980 [1955]) and Bernard Mishkin, *Rank and Warfare among the Plains Indians* (Lincoln, Nebr.: University of Nebraska Press, 1992 [1940]).

5   Jean Baptiste Trudeau, "Trudeau's Description of the Upper Missouri," *The Mississippi Valley Historical Review* 8: 149-79 (1921), 168; Elizabeth A.H. John, "An Earlier Chapter of Kiowa History," *New Mexico Historical Review* 60, 4 (1985), 385, 389.

6   Loretta Fowler, *Shared Symbols, Contested Meanings: Gros Ventre Culture and History, 1778–1984* (Ithaca, N.Y.: Cornell University Press), 24, 41–51.

7   Edwin James, "Account of An Expedition from Pittsburgh to the Rocky Mountains, Performed in the Years of 1819, 1820" in *Early Western Travels*, vols. 15–17, ed. Reuben Gold Thwaites (Cleveland, Ohio: Arthur H. Clark, 1905), v. 15, 220, 336; Fowler 1982, 309 n28; Hilger 1952, 140–41.

8   Mooney, *The Ghost-Dance Religion and the Sioux Outbreak of 1890*, 963–64.

9   Alfred R. Kroeber, *The Arapaho*, American Museum of Natural History Bulletin 18, 1902, 36–138.

Chapter 2:
The Four Hills of Life

10   M. Inez Hilger, *Arapahoe Child Life and Its Cultural Background*, Bureau of American Ethnology Bulletin 148 (Washington, D.C.: Government Printing Office, 1952), 4–6, 21–38, 42–43.

11   Alfred L. Kroeber, *The Arapaho*, 56, 58.

12   Ibid., 18–19.

13   Dorsey and Kroeber, *Traditions of the Arapaho*, 50–120.

14   Alfred L. Kroeber, *The Arapaho*, 151–58, 181–82

15   Truman Michelson, "Narrative of an Arapaho Woman," *American Anthropologist*, N.S., 35, 1933, 602

16   Hilger, *Arapahoe Child Life and Its Cultural Background*, 204–05

17   Fred Eggan, "The Cheyenne and Arapaho Kinship System," in *Social Anthropology of North American Indian Tribes*, ed. Fred Eggan (Chicago, Ill.: University of Chicago Press, 1955), 58–62.

18   Kroeber, *The Arapaho*, 158–206.

19   Ibid., 279–308; see also Dorsey 1903.

20   Kroeber, *The Arapaho*, 418–50.

21   Michelson, "Narrative of an Arapaho Woman," 609.

22   Hilger, *Arapahoe Child Life and Its Cultural Background*, 121.

23   Kroeber, *The Arapaho*, 206–10, 308–09; Mooney, *The Ghost-Dance Religion and the Sioux Outbreak of 1890*, 959–60; see also Loretta Fowler, *Arapahoe Politics, 1851–1978: Symbols in Crises of Authority* (Lincoln, Nebr.: University of Nebraska Press, 1982), 108–09.

Chapter 3:
The Struggle to Survive

24   Fowler, *Arapahoe Politics, 1851–1978*, 21–66.

Chapter 4:
Making Adjustments: The Northern Arapahos, 1878–1964

25   Hilger, *Arapahoe Child Life and Its Cultural Background*, 43–44.

26   Fowler, *Arapahoe Politics, 1851–1978*, 67–223.

Chapter 5:
Assimilation Tested: The Southern Arapahos, 1871–1964

27   John H. Seger, and Stanley Vestal, eds., *Early Days among the Cheyenne and Arapaho Indians* (Norman, Okla.: University of Oklahoma Press, 1934), 54.

28   Ibid., 3.

29   Mooney, *The Ghost-Dance Religion and the Sioux Outbreak of 1890*, 776, 894–900.

30   Fowler, *Tribal Sovereignty and the Historical*

Imagination: Cheyenne-Arapaho Politics (Lincoln, Nebr.: University of Nebraska Press, 2002), 3–47, 67.

31 Donald J. Berthrong, "Legacies of the Dawes Act: Bureaucrats and Land Thieves at the Cheyenne-Arapaho Agencies of Oklahoma," in *The Plains Indians of the Twentieth Century*, ed. Peter Iverson (Norman, Okla.: University of Oklahoma, 1985), 40.

32 Fowler, *Tribal Sovereignty and the Historical Imagination: Cheyenne-Arapaho Politics*, 48–132.

Chapter 6:
Arapahos and the War on Poverty

33 Fowler, *Tribal Sovereignty and the Historical Imagination: Cheyenne-Arapaho Politics*, xxi–xxii, 180.

34 Ibid., xxii.

35 Ibid., 129, 133–36, 148–54, 156–88.

36 Ibid., 134.

37 Ibid., 252–61, 269–75.

38 Ibid., 96–97.

39 Fowler, *Arapahoe Politics, 1851–1978*, 228–29, 232.

40 Ibid., 234.

41 Ibid., 238.

42 Ibid., 236–37.

43 Ibid., 172–76, 228, 267–71; Geoffrey O'Gara, *What You See in Clear Water: Indians, Whites, and a Battle Over Water in the American West*

(New York: Vintage Books, 2000), 137–38.

44 Fowler, *Arapahoe Politics, 1851–1978*, 257–59.

Chapter 7:
Northern and Southern Arapahos Today

45 Fowler, *Tribal Sovereignty*, 134–35, 158–69, 261–62

46 "Survey of Social, Economic, and Housing Characteristics," Oklahoma: 2000, 401, 403, 407, 410, 416 and "Characteristics of American Indians and Alaska Natives by Tribe and Language," Wyoming: 2000, 47, 61, 68, 89 in U.S. Census 2000. U.S. Department of Commerce, U.S. Census Bureau.

47 Fowler, *Tribal Sovereignty*, 169–70, 180, 184–85, 188–89, 193–95.

48 Ibid., 174–79, 181, 220.

49 Ibid., 97–98, 266–68; *wyoshpo.state.wy.us/med-wheel.htm*

50 *Wind River News*, 1990–2001; O'Gara, *What You See in Clear Water*, 51, 74.

51 Fowler, *Arapahoe Politics, 1851–1978*, 95–96, 130–35; O'Gara, *What You See in Clear Water*, 31–32, 37, 39–41, 91, 163.

52 O'Gara, *What You See in Clear Water*, 56–57, 85, 174–78, 182, 192–93, 217–18, 232–33, 236–37.

53 *Wind River News*, 1990–2001.

54 Ibid.

55 Ibid.

56 Ibid.

agent—A person appointed by the Bureau of Indian Affairs to supervise U.S. government programs on a reservation and/or in a specific region. After 1908 the title superintendent replaced agent.

Algonquian language family—A group of languages, spoken by Indian peoples of northeastern America, the Great Lakes, and the Great Plains, that have similar grammatical and pronunciation patterns and related vocabulary. Algonquian-speaking tribes include the Arapaho, Cheyenne, Cree, Blackfeet, Narragansett, and Abenaki.

Allotment—U.S. policy, first applied in 1887, to break up tribally owned reservations by assigning individual farms and ranches to Indians. Intended as much to discourage traditional communal activities as to encourage private farming and assimilate Indians into mainstream American life.

artifact—Any object made by human beings, such as a tool, garment, dwelling, or ornament; also, any marking in or on the earth indicating the previous existence of such an object.

assimilation—Adoption by individuals of the customs of another, usually dominant, society; a means by which the host society recruits new members and replaces a subordinate society's culture. The United States, as well as most American Indian societies, gained new members in this manner.

band—A loosely organized group of people who live in one area and are bound together by the need for food and defense, by family ties, or by other common attributes.

breechcloth or breechclout—A soft piece of hide or cloth, usually worn by American Indian men, wrapped between the legs and held in place by a belt or string around the waist.

Bureau of Indian Affairs (BIA)—A U.S. government agency within the Department of the Interior. Originally intended to manage trade and other relations with Indians, the BIA now is charged with developing and implementing programs that encourage Indians to manage their own affairs and to improve their educational opportunities and general social and economic well-being.

civilization program—U.S. policy of the late nineteenth and early twentieth centuries designed to change the Indians' way of life so that it resembled that of non-Indians. These programs usually focused on converting Indians to Christianity and encouraging them to become farmers.

fee patent—The right to hold land as personal property, without restriction; land ownership.

Ghost Dance movement—A religious and cultural revival movement that spread among Indians in the 1890s and centered on the belief that non-Indian newcomers would disappear and the Indians' traditional world would return if certain rituals were performed. During the rituals, individuals might enter a trance state and see visions.

giveaway—A ceremony practiced by many Plains Indian tribes in which members of a family, represented principally by women, publicly distribute property to others in honor of a relative, to express their appreciation for receiving an honor, or to acknowledge the acceptance of a responsibility. Non-Indian federal officials and missionaries objected to giveaways because they believed the custom undermined adjustment to practices of free enterprise and personal saving.

gold rush—A large-scale migration, beginning in 1849, from the eastern United States to the goldfields of California. The major traveling routes of the gold rush crossed the territories of many Plains Indian peoples, including the Arapahos.

Great Plains—A flat, dry region in central North America, primarily covered by lush grasslands.

horticulture—Food production using human muscle power and simple hand tools to plant and harvest domesticated crops.

Indian Child Welfare Act—Passed by Congress in 1978, this act gave jurisdiction to tribal courts in adoption or foster placement of children in order to end discriminatory practices of state and county welfare agencies. If a child had to be removed from the parental home, priority for custody would be extended family members, then tribal members, then Indians from another tribe.

Indian Claims Commission (ICC)—A U.S. government body, created by an act of congress in 1946, to hear and rule on claims brought by Indians against the United States for unfulfilled treaty terms such as nonpayment.

Indian New Deal—Program inaugurated by the Indian Reorganization Act of 1934, designed to remove U.S. government restrictions on Indian traditions and to encourage autonomous development of Indian communities.

Indian Reorganization Act (IRA)—The 1934 federal law that ended the policy of allotting plots of land to individuals and encouraged the political and economic development of reservation communities. The act also provided for the creation of autonomous tribal governments. Similar legislation, the Oklahoma Indian Welfare Act applied in Oklahoma.

irrigation—The routing of water to dry land through ditches, canals, or other means in order to make cultivation possible.

medicine power—The ability to accomplish particular ends, such as feats of bravery in war or curing of illnesses, by invoking and controlling spiritual powers.

Offerings Lodge—An Arapaho religious ritual whose participants have vowed to sacrifice through prayer, fasting, and other means in return for supernatural aid, and whose ceremonies dramatize events of creation.

oral tradition—The practice of preserving and passing on tribal history and mythology through the telling of stories.

peyote—A button or growth of the mescal cactus, native to Texas, New Mexico, Arizona, and the northern Mexican states, that is used as the vehicle, or channel, for prayer in several American Indian religious practices.

polygyny—A society's marriage custom in which a man may have more than one wife; a man's wives are often members of the same family, usually sisters.

powwow—An Indian social gathering that includes feasting, dancing, rituals, and arts and crafts displays, to which other Indian groups as well as non-Indians are now often invited.

Quakers—The familiar name for members of the Religious Society of Friends, a mystical and pacifist group founded in England by George Fox in the seventeenth century. Quakers were active in efforts to manage Indian agencies during the nineteenth century.

reservation or reserve—A tract of land set aside by treaty or executive order for Indian occupation and use.

Sun Dance—See Offerings Lodge.

tribe—A society of people consisting of several or many separate communities united by kinship, culture, language, and such other social factors as clans, religious organizations, and economic and political institutions. Many Indian tribes are federally recognized sovereign entities; others are seeking recognition.

trust—The relationship between the federal government and many Indian tribes, dating from the late nineteenth century. Government agents managed Indians' business dealings, including land transactions and rights to natural resources, because the Indians were considered legally incompetent to manage their own affairs. The trust relationship obligated the federal government to protect Indian resources and interests.

vision quest—A fast and vigil undertaken by Indian teenagers (usually boys but occasionally girls as well) and adults in the hope of contacting a supernatural being who might guide and protect the vision seeker through life. The vigil usually required extended solitude and fasting outdoors at a distance from the community.

Books

Anderson, Jeffrey D. *The Four Hills of Life: Northern Arapaho Knowledge and Life Movement*. Lincoln, Nebr.: University of Nebraska Press, 2001.

———. *One Hundred Years of Old Man Sage: An Arapaho Life*. Lincoln, Nebr.: University of Nebraska Press, 2003.

Annual Reports of the Commissioner of Indian Affairs. Washington, D.C.: Government Printing Office, 1846–1904.

Bass, Althea. *The Arapaho Way: A Memoir of an Indian Boyhood*. New York: Clarkson N. Potter, Inc., 1966.

Berthrong, Donald J. *The Cheyenne and Arapaho Ordeal: Reservation and Agency Life in the Indian Territory*. Norman, Okla.: University of Oklahoma Press, 1976.

———. "Legacies of the Dawes Act: Bureaucrats and Land Thieves at the Cheyenne-Arapaho Agencies of Oklahoma." In *The Plains Indians of the Twentieth Century*, edited by Peter Iverson, 31–53. Norman, Okla.: University of Oklahoma, 1985.

Dorsey, George A. *The Arapaho Sun Dance*. Field Columbian Museum Anthropological Series 4, 1903.

———, and Alfred L. Kroeber. *Traditions of the Arapaho*. Field Columbian Museum Anthropological Series 5, 1903.

Eggan, Fred. "The Cheyenne and Arapaho Kinship System." In *Social Anthropology of North American Indian Tribes*, edited by Fred Eggan, 35–95. Chicago, Ill.: University of Chicago Press, 1955.

Ewers, John C. *The Horse in Blackfoot Indian Culture with Comparative Material from Other Western Tribes*. Washington, D.C.: Smithsonian Institution Press, 1980 [1955].

Fowler, Loretta. "Arapaho." In *Handbook of North American Indians*, v. 13, pt. 2, edited by Raymond J. DeMallie. Washington D.C.: Smithsonian Institution Press, 2000.

———. *Arapahoe Politics, 1851–1978: Symbols in Crises of Authority*. Lincoln, Nebr.: University of Nebraska Press, 1982.

———. "The Arapahoe Ranch: An Experiment in Cultural Change and Economic Development." *Economic Development and Cultural Change* 21, 3 (1973): 446–64.

———. *Shared Symbols, Contested Meanings: Gros Ventre Culture and History, 1778–1984.* Ithaca, N.Y.: Cornell University Press, 1987.

———. *Tribal Sovereignty and the Historical Imagination: Cheyenne-Arapaho Politics.* Lincoln, Nebr.: University of Nebraska Press, 2002.

Hafen, LeRoy R., ed. *Pike's Peak Gold Rush Guidebooks of 1859.* Glendale, Ariz.: Arthur H. Clark, 1941.

Hilger, M. Inez. *Arapahoe Child Life and Its Cultural Background.* Bureau of American Ethnology Bulletin 148. Washington, D.C.: Government Printing Office, 1952.

Hosmer, Brian. "'Dollar a Day and Glad to Have It': Work Relief on the Wind River Indian Reservation as Memory." In *Native Pathways: American Indian Culture and Economic Development in the Twentieth Century*, 283–307. Boulder, Colo.: University Press of Colorado, 2004.

James, Edwin. "Account of an Expedition from Pittsburgh to the Rocky Mountains, Performed in the Years of 1819, 1820." In *Early Western Travels*, vols. 15–17, ed. Reuben Gold Thwaites. Cleveland, Ohio: Arthur H. Clark, 1905.

John, Elizabeth A.H. "An Earlier Chapter of Kiowa History." *New Mexico Historical Review* 60, 4 (1985): 379–97.

Kroeber, Alfred L. *The Arapaho.* American Museum of Natural History Bulletin 18, 1902.

Lavender, David. *Bent's Fort.* New York: Doubleday and Company, 1954.

Mann, Henrietta. *Cheyenne-Arapaho Education, 1871–1982.* Niwot, Colo.: University Press of Colorado, 1997.

Michelson, Truman. "Narrative of an Arapaho Woman." *American Anthropologist*, N.S., 35, 1933: 595–610.

Mishkin, Bernard. *Rank and Warfare among the Plains Indians.* Lincoln, Nebr.: University of Nebraska Press, 1992 [1940].

Mooney, James. *The Ghost-Dance Religion and the Sioux Outbreak of 1890.* Fourteenth Annual Report of the Bureau of American Ethnology. Washington, D.C., 1896.

O'Gara, Geoffrey. *What You See in Clear Water: Indians, Whites, and a Battle over Water in the American West.* New York: Vintage Books, 2000.

Powers, William K. *War Dance: Plains Indian Musical Performance.* Tucson, Ariz.: University of Arizona, 1980.

Salzmann, Zdenek. *The Arapaho Indians: A Research Guide and Bibliography.* New York: Greenwood Press, 1988.

Seger, John H., and Stanley Vestal, eds. *Early Days among the Cheyenne and Arapaho Indians.* Norman, Okla.: University of Oklahoma Press, 1934.

Sutter, Virginia. *Tell Me, Grandmother: Traditions, Stories, and Cultures of Arapahoe People.* Boulder, Colo.: University Press of Colorado, 2004.

Trenholm, Virginia Cole. *The Arapahoes, Our People.* Norman, Okla.: University of Oklahoma Press, 1970.

Trudeau, Jean Baptiste. "Trudeau's Description of the Upper Missouri." *The Mississippi Valley Historical Review* 8: 149–79 (1921).

Wind River News, 1990–2001. Lander, Wyoming.

Websites

Cheyenne-Arapaho Tribes of Oklahoma
http://www.cheyenne-arapaho.org/

Arapaho Language
http://www.native-languages.org/arapaho.htm

The Northern Arapaho Tribe
http://www.northernarapaho.com/

Arapaho Business Council
http://tlc.wtp.net/arapaho.htm

Wind River Reservation
http://www.wind-river.org/reservation.asp

Wind River Tribal College
http://www.wrtribalcollege.com/

page:

Loretta Fowler, Ph.D., is a professor of anthropology at the University of Oklahoma. She has been a fellow of the Smithsonian Institution and the D'Arcy McNickle Center for the History of the American Indian at the Newberry Library. She is the author of several articles and books on Plains Indians, including *Arapahoe Politics, 1851–1978: Symbols in Crises of Authority* (1982); *Shared Symbols, Contested Meanings: Gros Ventre Culture and History, 1778–1984* (1987); *Tribal Sovereignty and the Historical Imagination: Cheyenne-Arapaho Politics* (2002); and *The Columbia Guide to American Indians of the Great Plains* (2003).

Ada E. Deer is the director of the American Indian Studies program at the University of Wisconsin–Madison. She was the first woman to serve as chair of her tribe, the Menominee Nation, the first woman to head the Bureau of Indian Affairs in the U.S. Department of the Interior, and the first American Indian woman to run for Congress and secretary of state of Wisconsin. Deer has also chaired the Native American Rights Fund, coordinated workshops to train American Indian women as leaders, and championed Indian participation in the Peace Corps. She holds degrees in social work from Wisconsin and Columbia.